Passion for God

Passion for God: Theology in Two Voices

Jürgen Moltmann
Elisabeth Moltmann-Wendel

Introduction by
M. Douglas Meeks

Westminster John Knox Press
LOUISVILLE • LONDON

Scripture quotations from the New Revised Standard Version of the Bible are copyright © 1989 by the Division of Christian Education of the National Council of the Churches of Christ in the U.S.A. and are used by permission.

Scripture quotations from the Revised Standard Version of the Bible are copyright © 1946, 1952, 1971, and 1973 by the Division of Christian Education of the National Council of the Churches of Christ in the U.S.A. and are used by permission.

Jürgen Moltmann's essay "Globalization, Terrorism, and the Beginning of Life" is adapted by permission of Chalice Press from a previous version printed in *Strike Terror No More*, copyright © 2001.

Book design by Sharon Adams
Cover design by Lisa Buckley

First edition
Published by Westminster John Knox Press
Louisville, Kentucky

This book is printed on acid-free paper that meets the American National Standards Institute Z39.48 standard. ∞

PRINTED IN THE UNITED STATES OF AMERICA

03 04 05 06 07 08 09 10 11 12 — 10 9 8 7 6 5 4 3 2 1

Library of Congress Cataloging-in-Publication Data

Moltmann, Jürgen.
    Passion for God : theology in two voices / Jürgen Moltmann, Elisabeth Moltmann-Wendel ; introduction by M. Douglas Meeks.—1st ed.
        p. cm.
    Includes bibliographical references.
    "Featuring the 2002 Cole Lectures at Vanderbilt Divinity School."
    ISBN 0-664-22703-1 (alk. paper)
    1. Theology, Doctrinal—History—20th century.   I. Moltmann-Wendel, Elisabeth.   II. Title.

BT28.M624 2004
230'.044—dc21   2003053756

Contents

Introduction

M. Douglas Meeks

Christian history has produced few examples of married couples who are both world-renowned theologians. For over fifty years the marriage of Elisabeth Moltmann-Wendel and Jürgen Moltmann has harbored a fruitful theological partnership. This book provides a vivid insight into this partnership and the significance of their theologies. The main essays were given as the Cole Lectures at Vanderbilt University Divinity School and at St. Paul School of Theology in September 2002. The essays and meditations collected here look back to primary theological contributions of Jürgen and Elisabeth just as they open up new challenges for theology.

This celebrated partnership began in 1948 as the two young theology students met at Göttingen University. Jürgen arrived after having spent three years as a prisoner of war, during which time he was converted to Christianity. Elisabeth arrived from Potsdam, her birthplace and the city in which her family continued to live during the separations of the Cold War. From the beginning they were united in a love for theology. Jürgen had been raised

1

in a well-educated secular family and had come to faith after narrowly escaping death as a seventeen-year-old soldier in Hamburg and suffering despair as a prisoner of war. Elisabeth, who had been raised in a Christian family and shaped by the "underground church" Bible studies of the Confessing Church, began her theological studies in Berlin in 1945. At Göttingen they wrote their dissertations with the same *Doktorvater*, Otto Weber, and began a lifetime of lively theological exchange.

Since then their thought has shown profound similarities of spirit and common commitments and yet striking differences of theological emphasis. The difference in tonality may be partly due to "his and her" perspectives, or it could reflect the fact that Elisabeth came originally from a more Lutheran background while Jürgen has identified with the Reformed traditions. Differences also spring, of course, from their peculiar theological vocations: His as a leading ecumenical theologian in the esteemed Protestant Faculty of Tübingen University and hers as the leading feminist theologian in central Europe. In any case, they have always relished the spice of their differences and have sought to keep these differences alive within a deep mutual respect.

The commonalities of their theologies, however, are unmistakable. They are both theologians of reconciliation, always seeking fresh ways to speak of God's *shalom* coming to rest on earth. They are theologians of peace within the conflicts of the modern and postmodern world. They are ecumenical theologians in the broadest sense of the term. Their theologies flourish on the borders. They search out encounters with those who are culturally and politically different. They pay attention to what happens at the margins. They understand that the mode of theology is conversation, and their theologies reveal that they have listened as much as they have talked. Above all, they are theologians of life. They follow the Spirit who quickens dead bodies and wilted spirits and refuses to give over the creation to death. They are guided by the Spirit who seeks God's glory in the most unexpected places, among the humiliated, nameless, and powerless. In their thought, the Spirit of life weaves through the differences and makes the intellectual dance of this couple all the more inviting.

Several themes appear throughout the essays and meditations that follow: (1) suffering, violence, and God, (2) the cross of Jesus, (3) embodiment, (4) spirituality, and (5) friendship.

Suffering, Violence, and God

There is only one real subject matter of theology: God. At the beginning of modernity many Enlightenment thinkers were convinced that religion and "God" would disappear from public life. For a long time theology was wrapped up in the question of secularization. But it became clear in the last half of the twentieth century that we live in the most religious epoch in human history. Furthermore, there has never been a time that has been more religiously dangerous. Thus, theology has rediscovered its subject matter and has simultaneously become aware that unquestioned God-talk is what makes religion so dangerous. Language about God can camouflage or sanctify the interests of the powerful against the weak. It can be a mechanism for serving the interests of the masters and masking the pain of the victims. Therefore, theology should detect and expose God-talk that leads to coercion and suffering.

Both Moltmann and Moltmann-Wendel have been concerned throughout their careers about concepts of God that have contributed to domination. The God who is depicted as an omnipotent emperor leads to dominative and hierarchical relationships in church and society. Both theologians struggle against the forms of coercion and exploitation, especially that of powerful white males, that wreaked havoc on the world in the twentieth century and have not abated at the beginning of the twenty-first century. Because God-talk is so closely connected in the West to sovereign authority, unity, order, subordination, and obedience, it can easily be exploited for the subjugation of human beings and the degradation of nature. From the perspective of his political theology and her feminist theology, both seek the end of the hierarchical-patriarchal age.

If not from the models of human power, where then should images of God come from? For Jürgen, God-language springs from the narratives of Israel and of Jesus, but in the end they have to be crucified, that is, judged according to the presence of the triune God in the cross of Christ. Elisabeth's feminist theology vies against the archetype of the Father that condones violence to women, creation, and other religions. She works against images of dependency for women that came out of obedience to the Father and that have submitted women to the danger of perpetual childhood. For images of God, she turns toward the life of Jesus and his affirmation of life and calls upon the Wisdom, Synoptic, and Johannine traditions to create a friendship theology. The strongest tension between the two theologians is in the question of suffering and the cross.

The Cross of Jesus

Jürgen Moltmann's *The Crucified God* is without doubt one of the theological classics of the last half of the twentieth century. In his essay "*The Crucified God:* Yesterday and

Today," Moltmann looks back on the thirty years since the book was published in German in 1972. Luther said that all theology begins with suffering. Perhaps since Luther no theologian has taken this dictum so seriously as Moltmann. This book steadfastly gazes at the godforsakenness of the victims and the godlessness of the guilty in the violence and suffering of the twentieth century and refuses to speak of God except in the presence of these realities. It is Moltmann's most passionate book. In it a German tries to come to grips with the question: How can one believe in God after Auschwitz? In the face of such godforsakenness and godlessness, where is God? Does God share our suffering? Moltmann argues that for Christians, believing in God after Auschwitz is tantamount to believing in God after the crucifixion. The central God-question for Christians is uttered by Jesus on the cross: "My God, why have you forsaken me?"

What does the cross mean for God? Is God a transcendent and untouchable stage manager, or is God in Christ in the midst of world tragedy? With his claim that the death of Christ takes place in the innermost nature of the triune God, Moltmann reopened for our time the question of whether God is capable of suffering. Much of Christian theology has followed the "apathy axiom," according to which God's divinity lies in God's essential inability to suffer. This is what distinguishes God from human beings who are subject to suffering, transience, and death. But if God were fundamentally incapable of suffering, God would also be incapable of love. An impassible, immovable, uncompounded, and self-sufficing God does not go outside of God's self to suffer with the other, with God's creatures. Accordingly, God is not involved in Christ's passion. If Christ's passion is merely a human tragedy, there is no redeeming power in it. Salvation then is portrayed as the deification of human beings by means of the incarnation. If we become immortal, we also become impassible. This view of God undergirds the notion of the modern human being who understands apathy as power, as not having to suffer with the sufferings of others.

In the cross, however, God opens God's self for suffering. Why did God take the suffering of Christ on God's self? God does not suffer out of a deficiency of being but for God's love of creation, which is an overflowing abundance of God's being. Thus, the alternative to essential impassibility or fateful subjection to suffering is *active* suffering. For whom did Jesus die? For Moltmann the answer to this question issues in a double-sided Christology: solidarity and reconciliation. God suffered the death of Jesus in the cross for both the godless and the godforsaken, both the evildoers and the victims. A "solidarity Christology" pictures Christ the brother of victims beside us in our suffering and abandonment (see Phil. 2:7–8). Christ brings God's fellowship to those who are humiliated and emptied of their identity, to the "disappeared" of our belligerent world. A "reconciliation Christology" renders Jesus as the redeemer of the guilty, as the one whose vicarious suffering is the reconciliation of sinners. Without God's forgiveness of sins, the guilty cannot love because they cannot be freed from their past. Reconciliation happens as a communal event between God, the perpetrators, and the victims. Both sides of Christology—solidarity with victims and forgiveness of sinners—belong together for the redemption of the world.

From her feminist perspective, Elisabeth Moltmann-Wendel raises serious questions about the motifs of suffering and cross in Christian theology. She is suspicious of any theological move that issues from or moves toward sacrifice, since sacrifice and self-surrender have meant

repression and oppression of women. Therefore, she assid-
uously presses questions about the role of the cross and
death of Jesus. She is troubled about the way Jesus' death
interpreted as atonement for sins has produced one sacrifice after another. Theology should no longer glorify suffering; women should no longer be provoked to accept
suffering and sacrifice. She wants to remove any sense of
sadomasochism, passivity, and sacrificial mentality in
Jesus' death and replace this with Jesus' active devotion to
life. Her question is how to bring women to the power
that will give them self-determination. The New Testament message is the end of sacrifice and violence. Jesus'
death is a sign of devotion to his followers. His death is
self-determined. He dies for friends for whom he is a living example of justice.

Elisabeth, too, wants to speak of Jesus' Father's own
involvement in Jesus' death understood as freedom and
power of self-giving love. But this must be in terms of a
model of freely chosen dedication or self-surrender that
could make human life more relaxed and resolute. Therefore, Elisabeth searches the life-oriented traditions of the
past. Could the cross be interpreted as the "tree of life"?
Could the horizon of interpreting the cross be "natality"
rather than "mortality"? Then the cross would point to
being born as a never-ending desire for a new beginning.

In one of her essays Elisabeth poses the interesting
question, "Do women believe differently?" She comes to
the conclusion that women do not believe differently but
that they believe holistically. In her book *Rediscovering
Friendship*, she is critical of an overly aggressive feminist
theology that has "banished from its language and
thought all modes of behavior like acceptance, tolerance,
suffering, self-surrender, endurance and humility" (44).
Women, she argues, should reclaim the cross of Christ for

their own existence. The friendship theology she is developing does not reduce Jesus' death in favor of a new ethics. Rather, "it takes up the theology of the cross without dismissing it and interprets it out of existential experience. It offers new images which allow for understanding the life of Jesus as a friend's life, concretely experiencing his effort for justice and filling the theology of the cross, which has become so abstract, with new life."

Embodiment

Both Moltmann-Wendel and Moltmann have been major contributors to a new theology of creation that emphasizes embodiment and life with nature. Their theologies criticize the distancing of God and develop the theme of God's dwelling on the earth. Elisabeth shows in her essays in this book how women want to see God's reality brought back to earth, making God real in the world. Feminist theology is seeking a wide spectrum of experiences of God in the realms of personal relationships, politics, and ecology. Elisabeth's friendship theology treats the incarnation by speaking in fresh ways of God's embodiment and physicalness.

This view of embodiment asks for a humility about and acceptance of the finitude of the human body, but it opposes all forms of docetism and hostility toward the body. A male view of the mastery of the body as expressed in sports sometimes considers the body an enemy that must be conquered. The massive cosmetics industry does not reflect a love of body as much as a fear of aging. These views of the body deliver it over to manipulation and eventually lifelessness. A Christian perspective would understand the human body as fragile but nevertheless as an energy field of enormous possibilities of healing and rejuvenation. Elisabeth urges women and men not to leave their bodies behind in an escape to the intellect. Rather, they should understand with the body; there is no bodiless logic.

Theology also should learn that our faith is embedded in the body. In her meditation on the Markan account of the woman with a flow of blood, Moltmann-Wendel speaks movingly of one of her major themes: experiencing God physically. She considers this narrative as a women's passion story, a way of presenting the life-giving presence of Jesus. This story focuses on the body of Jesus. It is an intimate, physical, and mysterious event and points to the fact that Jesus' relation with others was one of bodily touching. The woman knows that she has been healed when she touches Jesus, and he knows that a healing power has gone out of his body. Streams of living and healing water flow from Jesus' body. Jesus leads a life-loving and life-giving physical life among the people. He is not incorporeal: "This is my body."

Moltmann-Wendel connects "This is my blood of the new covenant given for you" with the bodily communication that goes out of a vital human body and passes into the woman who is dying for loss of blood. But she points out that healing also comes from the woman's yearning to be a whole and healthy body and from her initiative in approaching Jesus. In moving toward Jesus, breaking taboos by touching him, the woman makes herself open to the flow of energy. She steps away from what makes her suffer alone and actively searches for what will make her well.

Spirituality

In his sermon "Praying with Open Eyes," Moltmann speaks of the kind of spirituality needed in the new age of anxiety after the terrorist attacks of September 11, 2001. In the 1980s and 1990s there was a widespread sense that the

American way of economy was fated to spread everywhere in the world. What could stop the McDonaldization of the world? A sense of satiation and self-satisfaction appeared in the first world, whereas many people in Africa, Asia, and Latin America experienced the juggernaut of globalization as a kind of everyday terror. The terrorism of which everyone became conscious on September 11 is a kind of counterfate to globalization. Now governments issue regular warnings of the possibility of terror, and this is leading to a debilitating inner terror. Moltmann's essay "Globalization, Terrorism, and the Beginning of Life" reflects on the Christian eschatology that must oppose the fanatic apocalypticism loosed in Christianity, Islam, and Judaism.

According to Moltmann, this new world condition in the faces of Globalization and Terrorism requires a new way of praying, with open eyes and hands and raised heads. It is the way Jesus prayed in Gethsemane when he was faced with terror. We live in a time of trembling and fear, when a sense of danger from which there is no escape can lead us to a numbness that is a kind of "death before death." This "paralyzing sleep" leads to a loss of a sense of reality so that we live only in our illusions. Jesus confronts us as he did his disciples in Gethsemane with the call to wake up out of our petrification. In fact, Moltmann understands prayer in a messianic sense as "wakeful expectation" of God in which all our senses are made alert. Awakening, watching, and expectation are modes of prayer. We should pray with open eyes and hands because prayer means waking up to the world and perceiving the groaning of our fellow creatures. In order not to sink into a new abyss of despair we should discover the face of the crucified one in the face of the victims of violence. Prayer is at once participation in the sufferings of God and anticipation of the coming redemption of God.

Moltmann-Wendel argues that spirituality is not just for the breaking points of life but also for the longings, little fissures, and joys of everyday life. Living feminist spirituality is to slow down. Our lives in the information economy are more and more reduced to exchange value and all kinds of technique. We are beset on every side by consumerism. The illusions of our virtual society end in cyclical disappointments. Spirituality should be thought of in terms of concrete ways of resisting competition and agonistic living. It is a spiritual mode of life best called *friendship*.

Friendship

Elisabeth and Jürgen are well-known for their theologies of friendship. Elisabeth's main essay in this book, "Friendship—The Forgotten Category for Faith and Christian Community: A Perspective for the Twenty-First Century," provides a lively introduction to this theme, which she has treated in several books. She sees the emergence of friendship in the face of the systems of domination, coercion, and violence as nothing less than a question of the survival of human beings. She looks for the church as a community of friends in which men and women are no longer determined by the traditional division of roles but can live as equals.

The ancient and modern models of friendship among men do not manifest the power to live with a friend who is genuinely other. Therefore, Moltmann-Wendel turns to the friendship images of the New Testament. She believes these images are largely shaped by the wisdom tradition, which knows no threat or punishment mechanism.

Friendship with God is the heart of this theology. It evinces God's freedom and power as God's love and God's love as an overflowing fullness, a searching erotic love that comes to dwell among God's creatures. God's friendship is the power and encouragement to self-determination, self-love, and self-responsibility.

For Moltmann-Wendel, a friendship Christology will understand the incarnation and our embodiment in fresh ways. Her reflections focus on Jesus' table fellowship as Wisdom and its practices that dangerously changed the rules of society. This fellowship does not accent friendship with the like but with the stranger. It is a life not so much *for* the other but *with* the other. It is a life of joy in the other and of respecting the differences of the other as the basis of living together. As she gives body to these reflections in her view of the church as a community of friends, Moltmann-Wendel points to new ecclesial life-patterns and rituals for friendship, for giving the other space, and for practicing hospitality to the stranger. She argues that these ecclesial practices must open onto a new social model of friendship in which friendship is given the priority over the life-form of the family. Such a social friendship culture should reclaim *eros* and tenderness for the existence of women (and men). *Eros* and tenderness belong to friendship with God and are the realistic means of breaking through the barriers of class, race, and gender, and of rediscovering the holiness of the earth. Friendship is love for the creation. Being a friend means healing the endangered life of our neighbor and of the earth.

The writings collected in this book will instill again in countless people around the world, Christian and non-Christian, a deep gratitude for the friendship of Elisabeth and Jürgen and the fruit of that friendship in the love of the creation.

Chapter 1

Experiencing God Physically

Elisabeth Moltmann-Wendel

Translated by Marianne M. Martin

There are stories in the Bible that even until today have seldom been preached about. These are stories about theft, about murder, about rape. But these are also women's stories that rarely appear in the lectionary of the church. Mark 5:25–34 is one of these stories. It is an embarrassing story, a so-called woman's story, about a woman's disease, a gynecological case. What does this have to do with our intellectual Christianity? Many male commentators are uneasy with this story, even today. The well-known New Testament scholar Eduard Schweizer called it "shockingly corporal"! Many commentators avoid it and get annoyed by the apparently magical thinking: a body-to-body healing! What should that say to the enlightened Christian of today?

But let us look at the story again. Let us look at this story from a woman's perspective. A woman whose life is marked by disease needs help. A woman is sick, but not sick from a disease in which she experiences sympathy, care, and social contact. Quite the opposite—it is a social disease through which she experiences isolation, loneliness, even defamation. She suffers from hemorrhaging, a pathological hemorrhaging. This makes her impure, according to the laws of the entire ancient world. This means that everything she touches also becomes impure and that the people of her society are also forced to withdraw from her. Otherwise they too would become impure and would have to undergo many cleansing rituals. Burning sacrifices of thanksgiving are expensive and require much time. We do not know if this woman was married or if she is still married at the time of the story. We only know that she has lost her value as a woman. She also comes alone, without support or help from others—just as all the sick women in the Gospels do, while it is repeatedly reported that the men were brought or accompanied by others. Women go to Jesus by themselves.

This disease is described as having lasted for twelve years. Seen medically and biologically, this time span is impossible, according to a medical doctor I know. Anemia would have led to death sooner. Yet the number twelve has symbolic meaning. Age twelve is when a young person becomes mature, and here the point of maturity is mistaken, bled to death, passed over. Twelve is also the number that comprises heaven and earth (Three times four: Three is the heavenly number; four is the number of the earth ["the four corners of the earth"]). Twelve, therefore, is the number of completeness, a number which cannot be excelled. Twelve is therefore the endlessly long, unlived life of a woman who does not experience fulfillment, a life which suffocates in isolation and loneliness.

This disease has real economic consequences: All the doctors who were consulted failed. These were doctors whose fees were paid out of her own pocket. This woman was able to afford this. She did not belong to the lower class! She was always getting new information about new doctors whom she sought after and paid but whose treatments did not help her until finally her money was gone, until her husband and the family were no longer willing to pitch in, until she was dropped. What she went through in terms of medical treatment, drugs she swallowed, good advice she heard, is described in the text as "suffering." This word appears again in the Gospel of Mark in connection with the passion story of Jesus, that is, his suffering through betrayal, torture, and crucifixion. It is a strong word, a dramatic word, but also a holy word for us. The Bible does not shy away from using this word for the experiences, the pains, and the lostness of this woman as well. It is a word which should make clear to us the whole spectrum and the whole tragedy of this story. It is a story of suffering, a feminine passion story! The fate of this woman is painted with a few strokes: betrayed, lost in pain and loneliness, economically at her end, physically at her end. "My God, why have you forsaken me?" One could describe her situation as a life which is no longer a life.

We who have gone through many Christian social stations—religious education, confirmation class, sermons, to name a few—should listen to this story very carefully. Normally the biblical healing stories are explained in such a way that it is Jesus who appears as the great healer, who speaks a word to the sick ones and makes them well, so that they can get up, stand tall, and move by themselves.

He frees from leprosy, from demons, from bad spirits.

He is decisive,

Decisive is his word.

Decisive is his speech.

Decisive is the hearing.

Decisive is the divine power which moves to the people through God's Word.

But when we now look at this story, we see that actually the exact opposite occurs. There is a woman, sick, powerless, without money, all alone, and she is the one who takes action. She begins to move. She takes the initiative. She breaks the cycle that has repeatedly kept her down. She speaks with herself because she has no one else she can consult. And then she makes her way from behind, toward the miracle worker about whom she has heard. Some people, indeed some women, do not like the "from behind." But isn't that typically female? Or perhaps this is a soberly considered single chance not to be dismissed from the beginning as sick or as an outcast. But to do this, this woman, this sick one, must leap over all societal taboos. She must of course know that if she touches Jesus, she will also make him impure and that that will require many expensive rituals to reinstate the purity! But she only knows that there is a divine power, a healing power which can make her healthy. The last hope for her! She must touch it! And all the taboos she knows must be put aside.

I think that *she* is the actual miracle of the story. The miracle is that she can say this sentence to herself: If I can only touch his clothing, then I will become well! Miracles also happen through us when we break the chains of obligations that surround us and hold us captive, when we follow our conscience and act for our passions, when we follow our intuitions that have been suppressed in our superficial, rational culture and of which we are barely conscious anymore. "If I can only touch his clothing, then I will become well!" I see it like this: With these words she opens herself for the flow of energy that can come from the one facing her, from this Jesus in whom she has put all her trust. With this trust—opposed to all other human experiences—energies flow into her, energies which touch her, touch her body, and which heal her.

With this trust, she opens herself to God's power and to God's presence.

Then comes, for me, the most impressive sentence of the story: "And immediately the hemorrhage ceased; and she felt in her body that she was healed of her disease." What she had felt in her body up to this point was the blood—life's energy—flowing out, her body becoming increasingly weak, interest and vivacity drying up, the mortal fear that the body might fail one day. Then she experiences how something stays in her that belongs to her—her lifeblood. She experiences how something becomes stable, how her fragile body becomes whole again, how she becomes healthy, whole, complete with all her senses and organs and how she is no longer haunted by mortal fear, by powerlessness. She experiences her body, her self: God's good, whole creation! And with this, interest and vivacity return to her. The verb "to feel," used here, holds something of this interest and vivacity of life, of this love of one's self, of this sensual joy in one's existence.

Many women today see their own life's path, their own life story reflected in this story. They see how they wear themselves out, sacrifice themselves in order to make things right for others, for the husband, the children, the profession; how they are drained and their life-energy flows from them until they have used up all their reserves, until their personality is reduced. They see how their ego is dissolved by all the particular wishes and by all the rights and by all the intentions until every bit of self-confidence has disappeared. Many women say that during this process they did not feel themselves, that they had no feelings for their own needs, no feelings for their own rights. After such experiences, grief and depression remain.

Also, increasing numbers of men lose themselves in today's race for professional success and achievement.

They know only their goals but not themselves. They also are bleeding to death until one day they are startled by a life crisis, by illness, by unemployment, a death. Then they begin to ask themselves about their wishes in life, about their needs, about their vivacity. This miracle waits in all of us: that we break through our closed existence, that we speak to ourselves as this woman did, that we hear our own voice again and listen to it, and that we open ourselves like this woman.

An amazing process takes place here—completely without words—and in the process, a person opens herself for God's life-energy, which brings her back to life. This is a return of the creation, a new creation, a new birth, and it is an amazing process that waits for all those who have lost themselves and become drained, in that they open themselves for God's life-power and return to life. In the beautiful film *Antonia's World*, it is said, "One must live!" This is something which can begin in these persons, what has begun in this woman. "Your faith has made you well," says Jesus to the woman later on. This is no dogmatic faith, no church faith, no "solid" faith as it is sometimes ascribed to the so-called faithful of our church. It is much more the basic trust in the life-making energies of God in this world. They encounter us in the most different manners: They encounter us in people, in a conversation, in that which is opposite us. They encounter us in the events of this world. They can also encounter us in books, magazines, and even through television. But we must be open to these sources of energy, of life's power, which surround us and bring us back into life.

Some people will ask: What is with this Jesus? Which role does he play in all this? He is present, but he is oddly passive. He is important, but in the beginning he knows nothing of what is happening. He only feels, just like this woman, how a life-power goes out of him, and how a dynamic leaves him. He is amazed or even startled and asks, "Who touched me?" The disciples who are so often the misleading fools, of course, once again do not know what is going on. They give him the wrong advice until he realizes himself: It was the woman. Here he is not the all-knowing one, and the disciples even less so. He is not a God who strides omnipotently around the earth. He is pulled into a process he must first of all understand. He hears the story of the woman, and at the same time it becomes clear to him which healing powers, especially for such people, for such women, can emanate from him.

It is like a dialogue in which both parties are involved and in which both are surprised and realize what has happened to them. The truth—that big word in the Bible—is what they both experience about themselves. She now knows what it is to be healed, to be whole, to be well. She knows what health is. He knows which powers of God he has in him that can bring such excluded persons, such women, back into the human society. The encounter with the woman shows him the way he must go for this excluded one and for all the excluded ones, for all those who are different, for those who think differently. For the Christians of that time who recorded this story, Jesus was not impure. He stood above such laws. In the closeness to God in which he proclaimed and lived, such human-made limitations fall away. The purity laws of the ancient world did not count for the early Christian communities. Just as Jesus knew of but was unmoved by such rules, a new sphere of freedom was also opened for the women.

In a manner which cannot be imitated, Jesus then shows the woman the way she is to go. With this, he shows that in this situation, he is in a different position than the woman. He goes beyond this dialogue. "Go in peace," he says, "and be healed." We know *shalom* as an expression for peace. But *shalom* also means wholeness and health. It is the peace we can have with ourselves, our souls, our spirits, our bodies. But *shalom* is even more. *Shalom* also applies to our relationships to the world, our relationships to people, our relationships to nature. "Go in peace," therefore, means to the woman: Do not only be happy and satisfied with your body, which is again whole and healthy. Do not only be happy and satisfied with yourself. Also be whole and healthy in all that challenges you, be it people, be it the issues of your world, your environment, your society, or be it the problems which are at hand, the problems which await you. Your center is in you. You are good, whole, and healthy. Now you can also go out into the great, wide world and spread *shalom*, wholeness, and peace. You do not need to be caught in yourself and your reclaimed energies and powers. Quite the contrary: These characteristics challenge you to be active in the world. They shine forth just as my energies shine on you.

Then Jesus says a word to her: "Daughter." He says this to a woman who is perhaps as old as he is or even older. Bible translations in German have always made this into "My daughter." With this, they have created a hierarchical relationship between Jesus and this woman that does not exist at all in the original Greek. The address "daughter" comes from the Old Testament. This term means not only an individual person. It means, most of all, Israel, the daughter of Zion, and it points especially to all the women who, like the hemorrhaging woman, shall no longer be excluded because of disease or being different, or because of physical suffering or a conspicuous physical condition. "Daughter"—this expression includes all the women of this world who are to be freed. "Go, make peace with yourselves"—is the message today. Make peace with your bodies that you abuse, that you train, that you paint and style without loving, without developing this *eros* which is God's *eros* to us. Experience your bodies again, feel in them wellness and power, regardless if they are old or young. See them as good creations of God, who said once for all things that God created, "It was very good."

Early Christianity gave this woman and this story a place of honor—quite the opposite of how they have been treated since. In the Syrian city of Caesarea Philippi, a unique memorial was erected for her: Jesus was shown there as a physician, in the form of the Greek God Asclepius. At the base of the memorial was a medicinal herb, and in front of Jesus stood the woman. This memorial was then destroyed in the fourth century in connection with the persecution of the Christians. We have forgotten Jesus the physician who heals people of everything that makes them ill. This beautiful and wide-reaching image includes our whole physical, mental, and spiritual existence. Unfortunately, through our church-image of Jesus, that is, as the one who forgives sins, this healing image has been pushed into the shadows. Forgiveness of sins touches only a part of our existence—our consciousness, our moral substance—and this can leave us empty, split, cut up. *Healing*—the word alone can reach into the last threads of our existence and touch us deeply.

We should rediscover the medicine of the Gospels, the medicine of life which makes us able with our whole existence—with body, soul, and spirit—to love and to accept and to see, to love and respect life in its abundance. This means, concretely, to rediscover the endangered life of this earth more exactly, to call attention to it and to work to save it. This also means—thinking in terms of healing—to take small steps, because everything that heals takes time. This can protect us from illusions and disappointments. Perhaps we also need some new symbols in

Christianity: Not only the cross but perhaps also the Christ who blesses, and perhaps also a woman, Mary, who could come anew into the center.

In the intellectual development of Western Christianity, sins and forgiveness of sins have moved into the center, and for this reason, this story has never been brought to light. In the same way, the living Jesus with his stories, his life, his vital life, his relationships, his friendships, and his healing actions have always been placed in the shadow of the symbol of the dead and resurrected Christ. Paul thought he did not know Jesus in the flesh; unfortunately, many theologians of the Western world have followed his example. Death and resurrection moved into the center of Christian proclamation, and the cross and the crucifixion became the sole symbol of Christianity.

In the Eucharist, then, that which is broken, symbolized as the dying body of Christ, is passed on and venerated, and our Eucharistic celebrations have too often become, as women complain today, like a wake or a commemoration for our sins. Our Christianity has become incorporeal and removed from the body. The vital nourishment, the means to life—bread and wine—often are only symbolic signs that represent the death of Jesus but nothing more. Our history, however, which tells of the life-giving body of Jesus, is at the same time a story of the Eucharist. It points to Jesus' Last Supper and his statement "This is my body," in which this healing story is remembered. This is my body, my life, my life-loving healing, my body which makes all of you well, gives you life-powers as it gave the woman life-powers.

Recently a woman told me this little incident: A woman went to her minister and said that she wanted to take Communion but that she didn't have a black dress! The minister responded in a friendly manner, "A black dress is not necessary. The main thing is that you know that you have a black heart!"

I think that the center of the celebration of the Eucharist is not the death, not the forgiveness of sins, not a "black conscience." The center is the remembering of Jesus' life-loving and life-giving existence among the people. It liberates us from the attitudes of sacrifice and from false self-sacrifices. It breaks down the barrier to the life-loving God without whom we feel lost.

The real story of this woman can help us become a bit more real, and not to leave our bodies somewhere, to flee into the intellect and only have our soul exalted. The word *wholeness*, which no longer has a place in traditional churches and theologies, can once again find a place in Christianity. "Be whole, like your Father in heaven," said Jesus in the Sermon on the Mount. "To be whole"—this reminds us of ourselves. We are not only made of head, consciousness, and intellect; rather, head, consciousness, and intellect are embedded in a body out of which one is nourished—regardless if the body is old, young, sick, beautiful, or weak.

This Gospel story reminds us that we are daughters and sons of God, created out of God's delight and *eros* for us, and that nothing can separate us from God or God's *eros*. It reminds us that God's energies are under us and that we can open ourselves to them. To be whole reminds us, finally, that we are children of this earth, connected with one and all, and that we are responsible for all of life.

Jesus showed the woman her way back into life, into her future. He freed her to step away from that from which she suffered, what made her afraid, what made her lonely. Be independent and active and search for that which makes you well. God's healing powers are present everywhere, and you will again experience delight and love.

Chapter 2

Friendship—The Forgotten Category for Faith and Christian Community

A Perspective for the Twenty-First Century

Elisabeth Moltmann-Wendel

Translated by Marianne M. Martin

In 1991, a study with the title "Church as Friend-Community" was published in a Munich theological journal. This study, from Catholic New Testament scholar H.-H. Klauck, interests me because it investigates traces of concepts of biblical friendship that have been forgotten in theology and upon which traditionally brotherhood language has been superimposed. It is also of interest to me because at the end of this study, the author shares his experiences of revealing the topic of his study to friends and colleagues, who mostly reacted with a laugh or a reply such as, "That is completely utopian" or "There is absolutely no chance of realization for this." The author summarizes that in the present, church as a community based on friendship—a vision with New Testament roots—has no chance. Though brotherhood and sisterhood have been discovered again, the still more deeply buried tradition of friendship is just as necessary for the search for a satisfying and liberating social character of the church. But now New Testament studies, especially from the United States, show how strongly friendship images shaped early Christian thinking, not only in the Gospel of John but also in Luke and even in the Pauline epistles.

Friendship images have always existed on the edges of the church. I think, for example, of the Friends of God from the Lower Rhine, or the Quakers, who are also known as "Friends," and the World Council for the Friendship Work of the Churches, which is especially engaged in pacifist work. These groups appear on the edge of church and theology today: in the ecological-theological movement of Matthew Fox and in feminist theology, especially that of Carter Heyward, Sallie McFague, Mary Hunt, and Julie Stewart. These perspectives challenge traditional theology.

The contemporary social experiences of the Western world are forcing a new friendship structure that could also gain theological meaning. The encompassing study by Klaus-Peter Jörns, "The New Faces of God," reveals that the most important thing in life for one of the largest groups that he interviewed was not kinship but rather its self-picked group of friends, and that the faces of God in the faith of the people is the form of life which correlates to that which is evident in their areas of life. Social friendships and God's friendship are, accordingly, closely related, and in what follows I also want to view them in this close relationship.

At the end of a hierarchical-patriarchal age, we must ask how we today focus these different challenges on friendship, as well as on new forms of women's friendship. We must also ask if we do not run the risk of missing people in their present-day life situations if we do not once again pursue the elements of the biblical friendship tradition that have been kept hidden so long and bring them into association with their actual life circumstances of today.

In the first section of what follows, I want to look at social images such as the family that are influenced by our expiring patriarchal age. I will then confront them with the newly arising images of friendship. In a second section, I want to present the basic model of friendship that has come out of biblical research. In a third section, I want to draw some conclusions for the church and theology.

Social Images Today

In all religions, the family plays a leading role as the institution that guarantees fertility and reproduction, and with that, a visible evidence of the affiliation with the divine. Also, the central social model which has shaped the two thousand years of Christian theology and church, faith, and piety is the family. Family images illustrate the relationship between God and humans: God is the father, humans are the children, Christian men and Christian women are brothers and sisters. Notions of the family stand as models for the church structures: pope, father, and the "early church fathers" rule the church family. Believers are known as children, as sons and daughters of such fathers. Such religious families have accompanied us since our childhood. They give us security and confidence, like parents' love.

First of all, with the idea of family, we associate strong emotional images such as security and protection. A family gives a person the feeling of belonging without conditions. A family teaches experiences and its own values, which are only available to the family members. Family images are an important track on which images of God can be mediated. They make sense and meet one's own, often good, experiences. But family can also be experienced critically: as a place where dependency is experienced and where obedience is demanded, and where intimacy can become seclusion from others.

Such negative images have made their way into the foreground over the past decades, especially through feminist social research. Cracks have appeared in the picture of the family that has been kept intact so long. These cracks allow our social image of the family to be, first of all, critically seen, and second, also to touch on our theological image of the family. The fathers in the society have long been challenged by their children who have become detached, and the children have also included many other images of God next to the image of the fatherhood of God. The patriarchal functions in the churches have slid into the twilight, and Christian women and men understand themselves increasingly as responsible partners. With this, images that have been meaningful for a long time have come to an end. These images have completely shaped the thinking and acting of the Western world. I would like to clarify this critique in three points.

1. For a long time the image of the family was shaped by the idea that at its head stood a man who legally, socially, and economically determined the fate of the family. This could lead to the abuse of power, to dependency, and to other family members being treated as minors. This patriarchal model of the family can also be found in the house codes of the New Testament. Here the husband loves his wife, but she should respect or fear him (Eph. 5:22–24). This long stood as a symbol of Christian order. Even when Ernst Troeltsch tempered this patriarchalism into a "love patriarchalism," the archetype of the father as sovereign authority remained for Christian

ethics. The notion of God as father—who represents unity, order, and a system of subordination and obedience—has also constantly been fed by such images.

2. One of the most shocking findings of the past few years is just how much violence can develop within the family. Incest, rape, and abuse have been disclosed as matters within families. Feminist theologians have pointed out that patriarchal Christian symbols can legitimate such violence. An Argentine pastor, Mercedes Garcia-Bachmann, has therefore called the Christian churches to reevaluate such symbols: "In our societies," she says, "the image of father is connected with violence and hierarchical structure. How many women, who have been beaten, raped, abused from childhood on, can still believe in a God the father?" The image of the father who—according to the Pauline version—abandons his son and relinquishes him to a death on the cross, can contribute to the justification of the image of paternal violence, according to the perspective of some feminist theologians.

It seems important that theology no longer glorify suffering and that women no longer be provoked to accept suffering and violence. It also seems important that the traditional sacrifice theology of the Jesus story be replaced by a presentation of Jesus' active devotion to life. Through this, cross and death are not the main themes of Christology, but the life of Jesus gains a new accent and offers encouragement for life.

3. The American theologian and professor Sallie McFague, who is looking for new images of God, doubts that parental images can still cover the notions of many feminine and masculine experiences. "Many people today," she writes, "are not parents and do not intend to be. . . . In our society, the father-child relationship is no longer so central as earlier and it is unnecessarily limiting to conceive

personal models only in parental terms." Furthermore, parental images can emphasize acceptance, leadership, and order, but it is difficult for them to represent mutuality, maturity, responsibility, and cooperation. In this regard, we must ask if the growing number of singles in our cities can still be attracted to religious images that come from a world which does not have much in common with theirs.

The question now arises of whether we should expand our perspective from the traditional family images that reflect our relationships to God and the divine to other experiences? It is time that we become open to challenging trusted and—up to now—proven images and begin to search for alternatives.

In his study "The New Faces of God," Klaus-Peter Jörns learned, based on interviews with people of various groups, that the most important thing in life for one of the largest groups questioned is not the family but rather one's self-picked group of friends. Jörns calls this group the "Transcendental Believers." They are the ones who, in different ways, are open to religious questions. With the "God Believers," in comparison, there are still metaphors used that are strongly bound to the institutions of marriage and family. But, Jörns asks, what will happen here when the new partnership among those who are not legally married breaks down even more? Or what if this is spread out even in conservative Christian circles?

The trend to give connections among friends the priority and to see in them the reflection of all forms of relationships has emerged. "The Faces of God," according to Jörns, "shows a correlation between the faith of the people and their forms of life, as they are shown to them in their areas of life."

I would like to go one step further in order to understand friendship today. Our model of friendship has long been determined by Aristotle's model of friendship among men. It was the friendship of equals who wanted to come closer to the truth through intellectual dialogue. Even for Nietzsche, women were only capable of love and not this type of men's friendship. In the *German Unabridged Brockhous Encyclopedia* of 1988, such male alliances as the ritualized Greek youth, male friends, and blood brothers are still dominant in the article about "Friendship." And in Schiller's famous "Ode to Joy," this male perspective is immortalized ("Joy, you beautiful divine spark" [*"Freude schöner Götterfunken"*]). Here the highest happiness is described "to be a friend of a friend" and at the same time "to win a favorable woman." (Also in Christian traditions, the meaning of friendship is shaped by male models: the friendship of David and Jonathan and of Dietrich Bonhoeffer and Eberhard Bethge, to name a few.)

But where is the happiness of women and what does women's friendship look like? Women's friendship belonged to and still belongs for many in a "niche culture." These friendships have no social meaning. They are considered necessary but rather ridiculed relationships in which all frustrations can be vented on the friend and where a woman can look for consolation.

This friendship type has its roots in the Romantic tradition, when men and women discovered the strength of their inner selves. If traditional male friendship is shaped by Aristotelian paternal thinking, so women's friendship is marked by a more egalitarian culture, in which for all sexes a heartwarming relationship has become a new social model. But some women in this time have developed a new social friendship culture beyond the psychic emotional relation, and this is important for us today. Rahel Varnhagen demonstrated in her salon that women's friendships can also point to the equality of the sexes and can therefore be a prelude to democracy. At the same time, she named her relatives, brothers, and sisters-in-law "friends" and made it clear that friendship could replace the blood bonds. In the understanding of women's friendship, friendship as a political issue and freedom from the pressure of the family are important elements.

Women's friendship today sets other but similar new accents; public and private become connected in it. It thrives in the everyday, awakens unknown energies, and creates freedom from the pressure of family and an openness for same-sex love relationships for women and men.

We also find another new form of women's friendship: friendship as a new form of solidarity on the common basis of women's suffering, especially from male violence. This form of friendship overcomes national and continental boundaries and was of help in the Balkan conflicts of recent years.

Women discover friendship in several ways: friendship as political, friendship as freedom for other lifestyles, friendship as earthing—bringing it down to reality—as source of the discovery of one's own personality and a liberation from stiff lifestyles.

This once one-sided male friendship model and this one-sided romantic female model take on many more facets today.

Friendship in the Bible

Can such friendships become an equivalent to the family? Are there theological or biblical models for this?

I believe there are such models because the Bible exhibits a wide repertoire of images of friendship which, more closely examined, could have at one time offered a real alternative to the family model. In John's thinking, those who follow Jesus are called "friends," and Jesus understood himself, according to John, as one who gave his life for his friends. But at some time in the early church, the decision must have been made that Christians would not be called friends, but sisters and brothers. Therefore, the family model gained preference. Adolf von Harnack thought the sister and brother image expressed more closeness and warmth. I believe, however, that at that time a decision in favor of the patriarchal church structure was made. Sisters and brothers belonged to a family and had a father. Friends, on the other hand, form a community of equals without a special sovereign. Even in early New Testament texts, one can find a clear critique of patriarchal family patterns. For example, the Gospel of Mark says that those who have given up everything for the kingdom of God will find everything again: mother, children, sisters, brothers, houses (Mark 10:29–31)—everything except fathers! The early community of Christians saw themselves as a community of women and men but without the dominance of a father. Their ideal was the *familia Dei* (family of God), the family without hierarchical structures, the family of friends.

When we continue to follow the clues of friendship, we encounter texts of the Old Testament in which a great man, such as Moses or Abraham, is named as God's friend, that is, as a loved or chosen one. But we also encounter a long-hidden tradition of friendship in wisdom theology, where such friendship with God is more democratic. God is viewed as a male friend, Wisdom as a female friend (Prov. 7:4; Wis. 8:9), and those who follow her are understood as friends (Wis. 7:14, 27). In wisdom theology we find a relation to God in the form of friendship—a relation without hierarchical traces. Here friendship is the expression for happiness and fulfillment (Wis. 8:18) between God and

humans without ignoring the dark sides of human existence; for instance, Wisdom goes with Joseph into the dun-
geon, into the experience of godforsakenness (Wis. 10:13).

Furthermore, in the New Testament we find a kind of
friendship theology in the Gospel of John and in the Synoptic Gospels in the stories of the meals with outcasts,
who are called friends.

But the primal image for this tradition of sharing a table
with friends as described in the Gospels is found in Old
Testament wisdom theology, and that indicates hidden
feminine traditions of friendship. There Wisdom sum-
mons everyone from the streets to her richly adorned table:

> Wisdom has built her house,
>   she has set up her seven pillars.
> She has slaughtered her beasts, she has mixed her wine,
>   she has also set her table.
> She has sent out her maids to call
>   from the highest places in the town,
> "Whoever is simple, let him turn in here!"
>   To him who is without sense she says,
> "Come, eat of my bread
>   and drink of the wine I have mixed."
>
>   (Prov. 9:1–5 RSV)

Here Jesus and Wisdom are seen in parallel: At the abun-
dant meal there is fellowship, people eat their fill, and there
is understanding, comfort, renewal—a prefiguring of the
banquets of the reign of God (Isa. 25:6; Mark 14:25).

According to theological research, Jesus understood
himself as Wisdom, and the earliest Christology seems to
have been a "Sophialogy." For women, a feminine model
emerges here which once again makes it easier for them
to approach the story and the practice of Jesus: It is orig-

inally Wisdom whose significance and functions Jesus takes over. And it is important that Jesus' friendly action is expanded by Wisdom the householder, who issues an invitation, for she is wine steward, butcher, and cook. Here friendship takes on more life, becomes more concrete, practical, and vital. If one asks oneself who prepared the meals for the group around Jesus, a realistic picture emerges here: It was the women, the women householders and their women servants, who themselves had everything under control. Like Jesus, Wisdom does not celebrate the meal with close friends but with those who are remote, that is, strangers.

Jesus, who probably understood himself as such Wisdom, invited people to his table. He became friends with tax collectors and sinners. In the New Testament, being a friend and acting as a friend becomes concrete in the person of Jesus; to be a friend, which in the splendor of a community around the table encourages one to life's joy, finally ends in the devotion of a friend to such a friend.

This is "acting as a friend" that wants to end the injustice in a society and a culture, and with that, injures the rules of a society in a dangerous manner. It is an action as a friend that revolutionizes our bourgeois or romantic image of friendship!

It is important for women today to know that this action as a friend of Jesus' also included women who were tax collectors, sinners, and prostitutes. Further, Jesus' identification with Wisdom also gives many women today the right to see a friend in the man Jesus.

In the Bible, friendship has many faces and in no way favors an everlasting male friendship. Quite the opposite—the Bible overthrows this image.

Later, images of friendship with God and respective social friendship patterns emerged in the work of many theologians. We see these, for example, in Luther, Paul Gerhardt, and John Wesley, who once called God "the universal friend of all the families in heaven and on earth." However, the father-child model remained the decisive model for all Reformed theological approaches.

Conclusions for Church and Theology Today

If we combine the various images of friendship from Wisdom, Synoptic, and Johannine thinking, a friendship Christology and a friendship theology could result. Such is long overdue and could give necessary impulses for today. Four aspects appear to be important.

1. The social model of friendship based on freedom and equality are two notions which are not elements of the family model. A man or a woman decides for a friendship through free merit. Freely chosen decisions and not dependency are the characteristics of a friend relationship. If we stretch these thoughts to the relationship of God or the divine with humans, then a new relationship of God takes the place of old established images.

For a long time, our relationships to God were shaped by images of dependency that came out of obedience. Today we see in this the danger of a perpetual childhood in which it is difficult for responsibility, maturity, and self-determination to evolve and in which people today cannot fulfill their responsibility to the creation or fulfill their share of partnership with the creation. In light of growing technological abilities and possibilities of people, there need to be new religious values and also encouragement to self-determination and self-love in order to be prepared for new tasks in church and society. I do not think the images of friendship can completely replace images of the family, but rather that friendship images should appear next to the family images as helpful, necessary, and enriching.

2. Churches, liturgies, and many theologians are still influenced by the understanding that Jesus' death is an atonement for the sins of humanity. Critical theologians have pointed out for a long time that the atonement interpretation is only a later interpretation with very thin traces to the New Testament and that it should in no way be made into the norm. Many people, especially women, decline the sacrificial model because according to their perspective and life experiences one sacrifice only produces another sacrifice. Sacrifice is always connected with violence, and the New Testament only speaks of sacrifice in order to exclude it. The message of the New Testament is the end of sacrifice, the end of violence.

A friendship theology could be helpful here. Such a theology offers an alternative interpretation of Jesus' death. It understands his death as a sign of devotion to his friends. Accordingly, Jesus died not for our sins but rather for his friends, to whom he was a living example of a life of justice. There is no legitimating or glorification of sacrificial behavior to be read out of this story but rather a self-determined, justice-oriented life. This type of friendship theology does not, however, reduce Jesus' death in favor of a new ethics. It takes up the theology of the cross without dismissing it and interprets it out of existential experience. It offers new images that allow for understanding the life of Jesus as a friend's life, concretely experiencing his effort for justice and filling the theology of the cross, which has become so abstract, with new life.

3. According to Jörns's study, the face of God in the faith of the people correlates with the form of life as it shows itself in their areas of life. With this, the interest in

relationships and mutual attention which does not fall into dogmatic elements grows. But relationship with others does not mean individuals want to be alone or independent. It has to do with their desire to live in relationship with people and also with God—as far as they are still interested. A friendship model can gain new meaning here. It is exactly the new lifestyles that women's friendships open up that can set other accents. Not to be *for* others, but to be *with* others—this thinking becomes more and more important.

More than family patterns, such friendship patterns point to an important pillar in our relationship culture: the knowledge of the differences between people and respecting such differences as a basis of living together. God's friendship can also be an example of this.

As in any friendship, God can be the friend of closeness or intimacy, but just like any friendship, this friendship only has stability if the otherness of the friend is respected. Also, God as friend cannot be absorbed but rather remains God's self. Friendships that do not keep this basic rule have no stability.

In the past, family images have often proclaimed the unity and equality of Christians—male and female—and feared strangers. Today on an overcrowded planet, as Sallie McFague observes, the old ideal of friendship with strangers presses forward again: Friendship with strangers and those who are different as individuals and as nations and cultures. After centuries of hierarchical and polarizing models, such friendship models are needed for the survival of humankind: "If humans do not become friends, then they will not survive" (McFague). Friendship breaks through barriers of class, race, and gender. The fear of strangers that lingers in all of us could mellow into a curious, creative attraction for the other.

In such open friendship, the old and familiar must not be given up, but rituals, for example, should be reconsidered, revived, and expanded in order to give the other space.

If family symbols seduce people to remain childlike, dependent, and obedient, then friendship images encourage people not only to be self-confident and responsible but also to be open and curious. Churches whose basic model is friendship can open themselves to new life-questions and new people.

A saying goes that whoever is God's friend must be the enemy of all the world. This ill-fated saying unfortunately has its origin in the letter of James: "Whoever wishes to be a friend of the world makes himself an enemy of God" (Jas. 4:4–5). Such a friend-enemy relationship, however, has no other biblical background.

Sallie McFague has pointed out that in Hebrew thinking, the counter-concept for friend is not enemy but stranger. The stranger is therefore the potential friend. This idea then illustrates the table community of Jesus with these very different ones, these outsiders, these strangers whom he wants to make into his (female and male) friends. This image should also be the basis for thinking about Christian friendship.

4. An important aspect for a human-friendly church comes to us out of the theological work of women concerning friendship and women's friendship. In the past years, several works about this topic have appeared. In spite of their differences, they all indicate that the experience of friendship points to long-forgotten dimensions of God's physicalness, of incarnation. Women want to bring the wide spectrum of experiences of God and God's reality back to earth. This can include various realms of life: relationships, politics, ecology. Friendship offers

itself as a long-forgotten possibility of making God real in the world.

Here are some examples:

For the American theologian Carter Heyward, God is "the power in relationships," and this exists "between plants and dogs and whales and mountains and cities and stars. Divine beings drive us, long for us, move in us and through us and with us in that we recognize ourselves as humans and learn to love as human beings, who stand from the beginning in the relationships and are not alone." She calls this relationship friendship, and it encompasses God and the human and the whole creation. It is important for Carter Heyward to make God incarnate in such friendship in the world. In this way, incarnation takes place for her—in the past and today and repeatedly.

For another American theologian, Mary Hunt, women's friendships are a focus of interests, out of which impulses for the reacquisition of the symbol of the divine can be gained. In concrete actions, in community meals, in celebrations and rituals, and in actions for justice, something of the divine, of a friendlier world, becomes activated here. Hunt is a lesbian theologian, but her theology of friendship encompasses more than just women's relationships.

For a German, Catholic theologian, Hildegund Keul, the term "women-friendship" (*Freundinnenschaft*) takes a central place in her friendship thinking. In women-friendship, in connecting and uncovering unknown life-energies, women can give up their old roles of "keeper of the home" and become "creators of the world." In hearing and listening, in being heard, God is present as woman-friend.

For Sallie McFague, the world is God's body. The image of God's kingdom bound to images of the sovereign authority is no longer important for her, but rather this body of God as humans can experience it in their newly won corporeality, in their responsibility for the creation, and in a new understanding of the sacraments. In friendship with God and among one another, humans find their way back to a holiness of the earth, the matter, and to a living and an understanding of the incarnation that is not abstract.

In these different "earthings" from women—that is, the way in which they bring friendship back to the earth and make it concrete—dimensions of a creation theology, which we desperately need today, become visible. To believe in God in the creation may not remain abstract but must become concrete in rituals, in actions, in friendships that awaken the other to life, in an understanding of the Eucharist that makes us conscious of the holiness of the matter in our own energy that makes God real among us. Without these feminist earthing-models, friendship will remain abstract!

The contribution of women to God's friendship can change our understanding of a still distanced relationship of God to the world. Friendship then becomes a chance to understand incarnation anew and to experience it and to allow it to be reflected in all of our lives. Through this, Christian faith can be freed from dogmatic narrowness into a cosmic openness.

When we open ourselves anew to the old biblical topic of God's friendship:

> People will be encouraged through this to self-determination, self-love, and self-responsibility, a message which is so important for women and will change the traditional division of roles in the church.

Instead of the atonement theology that is a burden and so difficult for many, the life and death of Jesus can be understood anew from the perspective of friendship action and the love of friends. The commitment of Jesus' life moves back into the middle point of theological thinking.

The ideal of an open church-friendship becomes a way also to approach strangers with openness and curiosity. Friendship is a better image or orientation for the counselor than proclamation or service.

God and the divine will be retrieved in incarnate form to this earth in many experiences of friendliness and friendship. God's friendship teaches us to live in friendship with our bodies and in friendship with the earth and to once again make the earth into God's domicile.

Such a friendship of God is, however, not a dogma. It is an offer to experience one's self, God, and the world anew. It is an offer, in a rapidly changing world, not to stand still and look back but rather to put one's hand on the plow and to look forward. After a long way filled with mistakes, accommodations of societal hierarchies and the suppression of early Christian charismatic beginnings, it is now time for the church today to open itself to democratic-charismatic movements that are shaped by life-patterns based on friendship. In these, God can again be present as (male and female) friend, and the people can taste and see how friendly God is.

Literature

Jörns, Klaus-Peter. *Die neuen Gesichter Gottes: Was die Menschen heute wirklich glauben.* 2d ed. Munich: C. H. Beck, 1999.

Klauck, Hans-Josef. "Kirche als Freundesgemeinschaft." *Münchner The-
   ologische Zeitschrift* 42 (1991): 1ff.
McFague, Sallie. *Metaphorical Theology*. Philadelphia: Fortress Press,
   1987.
———. *Models of God*. Philadelphia: Fortress Press, 1988.

Chapter 3

Do Women Believe Differently?

Elisabeth Moltmann-Wendel

Translated by Marianne M. Martin

Many women have experienced God through a powerful, male-oriented church, and through a word-heavy minister. The question of one's identity as a woman, however, has remained unanswered in these male-dominated games of power. Many women have left this, in their eyes hopeless, institution. They have found identity and interest in life through other religions, through goddesses such as Innana, Isis, and Freia. Other women have searched for forgotten female traditions in Christianity and have rediscovered their identity and the lost feminine dimensions of God.

Images of God, which for so long were exclusively masculine, have been revealed also to be feminine: God with breasts who nurses, loves, nurtures, and cares for her children; God as an eagle mother, as a lover, midwife, friend; and most of all, God as wisdom. These images of God, which are securely anchored in the Old Testament and are important for many women, also show alternatives to traditional behaviors of God: Wisdom goes through the streets, calls to the people, and invites them to her table for wine and good food. This Wisdom tradition knows no punishment or threat mechanism. God-Wisdom is searching, erotic love. Whoever does not follow her throws herself aside. And Wisdom also accompanies people in all hopeless situations, as for example with Joseph in the well, I see three different approaches of women to the Christian tradition.

Christian Faith and Eros

For many women, it is important to see the behavior of the biblical women anew: Women do not run when Jesus is arrested, and they risk staying near the cross in order to accompany the enemy of the state to the grave and to care for his body in an appropriate manner. There must have been an erotic relationship, a friendship, between the women and Jesus which endured beyond his death. This relationship was passionately fulfilled by the early leader of the church, Mary Magdalene. Her preaching was said to be neither zealous nor demanding but rather based on existential experience and filled with sweet words.

This female character, who was filled with *eros*, friendship, and independence, according to the New Testament and early church writings, was later degraded to the "Great Sinner." Her own experiences of God could no longer be a model. In place of this, a new image of women arose: as sinner and seducer who could only be reaccepted through the grace of God. The rediscovery of Mary Magdalene's character which is not burdened with dreams and visions of motherhood as Mary, mother of Jesus, could become a model for a new leadership in Christianity: an independent woman, free from responsibilities of family and marriage, characterized less by age than friendship and abilities to create a new style of relationships.

Women today are rediscovering such a love of God and love to God. This love, shown in images and stories as the power of *eros*, as erotic power, is more than the power of *agapē*, this static, satisfied and controllable style of relationship for which Christianity decided. Instead of this, *eros* shows the overflowing fullness of God. It cannot be limited to one single image of God, neither that of the father nor of the mother. God is more; God can also be perceived in natural images and not only in social images. God has many faces—light, well, tree, water—all that which gives people life and makes them free to believe with all of their senses.

Many women today understand God to be the "power in relationship," and this also exists "between plants and dogs and whales and mountains and cities and stars," says the American theologian Carter Heyward. Such faith is not just "believing in something" but rather a movement which connects us with one another, with the cosmos and with God's wisdom, which is everything to everyone. God-*eros* allows us to experience the earth anew and helps us to string together the band of love among each other every day.

Rediscovering the Body

Through this, the Christian faith will also cause far-reaching changes in people themselves. *Eros* as relationship to God and the cosmos also affects the bodies of people, which in the Western tradition are often neglected or feared because of the drives that are housed in the body. Especially women who see themselves as part of the Christian tradition—in which they have been made into sinful, seductive daughters of Eve who actively participated in the fall—have begun to think about things differently. For these women, the body is no longer sub-ordinated to the spirit or the mind. They have rediscovered their own body rhythms and with these, often a secret potential of powers. They are learning to mistrust the medical assumptions that women's bodies are weak and unreliable. They have begun to understand and to love their bodies with their uniqueness.

Long ago, Swedish women formulated an impressive prayer of confession which stated that they did not love their bodies and did not respect their own talents and asked for God's forgiveness. With a new love for the body, women today are again seeing themselves as a creation of God, a perspective which disappeared from our understanding of faith long ago. This reflects the understanding of creation that is reported in the first creation story: that God saw everything God had made and it was good. These words of praise then repeat themselves in the healing stories of the New Testament. The people see how Jesus makes the bodies of sick people well again and they confirm this well-being with the same expression as in the creation story: "He has made everything well."

But it is a long process of rethinking and of changing one's life in which women are engaging themselves. For too long, women have learned in church and society that their bodies are a "service body," always ready to act and, in earlier times, to bear children and be fruitful. Even today, too much hostility against the body—this fascinating creation of God's—comes to us from society. For example, in sport the body is considered an enemy which must be conquered in order to achieve top performance.

Also, the constant medical preventive suggestions point to the enemy in the body, an enemy which wants to secretly eliminate me. Female doctors point out that the breast, a sensitive female organ, is actually only looked at, touched, and handled with mistrust by women. It is as if the secret adversary of my life hides in the breast! The cosmetic hints of how we are to shape, care for, and cream our bodies are not exactly images of love of the body but rather of fear of age and decay and the hardly successful desire to retrieve youth. It is, therefore, as history and our present culture show, a long way back to the body, to a holistic view of ourselves.

This way is easier when I make it clear to myself that it is a process which leads to the whole. Every direct route contradicts the process in which the healing of something which has been separated for so long should take place. There is also stagnation and resignation, standing still and backtracking in a process. But there can also be new discoveries: the miracle which can be seen in me and my body when a dozing talent, the energy which had previously not been released, comes forth. The body can become my friend instead of the secret enemy of my life's path. It can become the body to which I must listen and pay attention.

The body is an energy field of enormous scale. It is no longer a rigid container for my soul or even a cover for my intellect. But this becoming whole means different things for different women with different life stories. Some women discover the rights of their own sexual wishes which also results in perceiving their vis-à-vis holistically. Others experience joy when they realize they can feel while thinking and think while feeling, that they can understand with the body and no longer want to do bodiless logic. For some, the apparent triviality of their domestic work can now become a source of one's own judgment. There is a material spirituality that develops within daily work: daily work that is creative, nurturing, and fruitful for a community and in which the chaos is mastered.

There are women who in this connection speak of the incarnation in a feminine body. Because theology has been fixated for such a long time on the incarnation, and the old traditions of the inhabitation of the spirit in people had been forgotten, it seems to be the time to also see salvation embodied in women. Such becoming whole and being healed has, however, never had the goal of completeness. Quite the opposite: The fragmentary remains characteristic of this journey. But the torn, broken, and split off should be seen, and healing steps toward a whole should be taken. What such a "whole" means was expressed by the poet Rose Auslander (who died in 1988) with these fitting words: "to be bumped sore in all corners and to remain whole."

The creation energies of God in the lives of women, of humans, again becomes visible through such experiences of wholeness. In place of the confession that stifles many women—"I, the poor, misfortunate, sinning person"—comes the desire to carry these creation energies into the world. God became human, a whole human, and women are now redeeming this belief in their minds and bodies. Women do not believe differently—they believe holistically.

The Meaning of Life

According to the old tradition, hope of a life in the future world belongs to the primary components of the Christian faith. Christian eschatology, resurrection of the dead, and eternal life have been central elements of the faith up to today, even when they have undergone modern interpretations. But on these points, many women have clearly withdrawn from these traditional doctrines, and this withdrawal has not taken place quietly but loudly.

Women demonstrate that there is a life *before* death, and point to how often Christianity has avoided existing social problems and shoved the solutions into the life hereafter.

The attention believing women give to these problems has clearly and passionately been moved to this side of life. They see the central task of church and religion in the social problems of the present, and the sin of the past in not having been involved enough in suffering and the interests of humankind. God wants to live here, in a place of healing, where healing takes place.

The image of life, then, gains a completely new central meaning for women. There can be no mitigation through the prospects of a later, eternal life. Life is present here in its abundance and in all of its demands. God came into this world, and discipleship and religious existence must take place in this life. Martha's confession to Christ who came into this world (John 11:27) becomes concrete at this point. Life has many dimensions for women now. There is first of all the *societal life*, which is still defined by patriarchal social structures and in which women and minorities have been given neither human rights nor appropriate living space. The feminist movement began with these questions, and these only partly solved social issues still form the middle point of women's involvement. The struggle against violence has become a focus of action and reflection over the last fifteen years, as well as the experience of violence within the churches and religion.

A further dimension is *daily life*. Today there is a view of the world that comes out of appreciating everyday occurrences. Through this, much of what is invisible becomes visible: for example, the work of women in the home, which has been made invisible; or the significance and economics of domestic work, which has held no value in the women's movement for a long time. Also, the daily conflicts at home and at work belong to this complex: competition, mobbing, division of housework, new perspectives for children, and so on. The Brazilian theologian Ivone Gebara explains:

> The emphasis of healing in light of daily life does not mean that we deny all possibilities which open the perspective to the other side of history. The tension between the historical now which we are experiencing concretely and this other world of our tradition of faith and our hope can be endured. One must, however, pay attention to not emphasize the other world at the expense of the concrete history. The women have rediscovered the dimension of the daily life in history. With this, they have appropriated the tradition of their history and the daily meaning of the stories and parables in the Gospels. In the elementary things of life, in the encounters of friendship, the small joys of each day which are the source of a feeling of thankfulness and of receiving a gift, lies one's own spirituality.

Biological-physical problems also belong to this complex in increasing dimensions, especially in light of women's lives. A new orientation is needed concerning what the body of a woman actually is. This means a turning away from male perspectives, health reform, new technologies, and an independent style which is yet to be achieved, of dealing with individual bodies in a friendlier manner. Finally, to this complex also belongs the cosmos and nature, which just like women are also exploited and endangered and need an interaction based on friendship.

The interest and concentration with which women engage themselves in such questions of faith is unknown to many men who think traditionally. What traditionally has belonged to the field of ethics has been moved to the field of faith for many women. Here is where women make the decisions of religion and Christian faith. In their passion for immanence, they also believe to have solved the questions of transcendence. So it is only logical that the question of the resurrection is not an issue of transcendence for them but rather of immanence. Resurrection takes place for them in standing up against injustice. Resurrection must manifest itself as an uprising. For a significant group, discipleship means to resist unjust structures, and Christ's resurrection and ascension are seen as myths that divert attention from this earth. Ivone Gebara replaces the biblical Christian idea of the kingdom of God with the word *resurrection*. Later does not count; the here and now counts, the present experience of justice and fate and the desire for God in us and our world.

In my opinion, the most important differences to the prevailing religious tradition are to be found here. Women have articulated noteworthy differences to classical theology. There is, however, still much movement, and no final consensus has yet been made about a different women's belief.

The Cross Becomes the Tree of Life

One thing we should make clear in any case is that the interest women have developed for the concrete life is connected with a highly critical interest in the traditional core of the Christian tradition—cross and resurrection. Many have experienced the theology of the cross with their own story of the crucifixion of their person, their rights, and their interests, but this experience is inaccessible for others. Crosses, in the opinion of many, must be analyzed and overcome today. They should no longer be the defining symbol of a religion.

Certainly much speaks for the need to supplement the old symbols of Christianity, to expand them to include life-oriented symbols—the circle, the wheel, the manger —or to give a new interpretation to the cross as the tree of life, in accordance with an old medieval practice. Christianity's apparent fixation on death can be countered with knowledge of life-oriented traditions of the past. But we also need new impulses in order to break away from the patterns hostile to life.

The Jewish philosopher Hannah Arendt (who died in 1975) presents an idea helpful in this process. In contrast to the prevailing notion of mortality in Western thinking—the focus on death—she presents the idea of *natality*—having to do with birth—and suggests shaping Western thinking anew through this. Instead of being set on the linear and inevitable end of our life in death, we could use our being born as a never-ending desire for a new beginning and surprise as an orientation. With each birth, something new comes into the world. This worldview can again steer our view to the desire for life which stood at our very beginning. Instead of looking at the end, we could learn to look at the beginning and see a beginning that is not past but rather is new every morning and that can make our love to the world newly visible. Hannah Arendt based this life perspective in Christianity: "Unto us a child is born." This child says that we are also born in that all possibilities and abilities and all charms lie in the new beginning. Such a belief leads us directly back to Christian origins.

Natality instead of mortality; the tree of life instead of the cross. These are accents which women today are setting. These accents represent a change in paradigm that can be helpful not only for women. Here women have engaged themselves with their persons, their stories, and their experiences the most, and they have shown that they are not "different" and off-target but rather they are on-target and are rooted in the center of life: in the middle of a living faith, a belief in our unique life.

Chapter 4

Praying with Open Eyes

Jürgen Moltmann

Translated by Margaret Kohl

What else is Christian spirituality except watching and praying, watching prayerfully and praying watchfully? Prayer never stands by itself. It is always bound up with watching. Here I want to talk about the watching, which goes with true praying, and to which true prayer is supposed to lead us. Praying is good, but watching is better.

Modern men and women think that people who pray no longer belong properly to this world at all. They already have one foot in the world beyond. Strong men often think that praying is something for old women who have nothing left to them but the rosary or the hymnbook. It has become rather unknown that praying has to do with awakening, watching, attention, and the expectation of life.

It is true enough that our body language when we pray does not suggest particular watchfulness. We close our eyes and look into ourselves, so to speak. We fold our hands. We kneel down and lower our eyes—even cast ourselves down with our faces to the ground. No one who sees us would get the impression that this is a collection of especially watchful people. Isn't it rather blind trust in God which is expressed in attitudes of prayer and meditation like this? Why do we shut our eyes? Don't we need much more prayer with open eyes and raised heads? But for what are we supposed to watch? For whom are we supposed to watch? And whom or what shall we expect?

"Could You Not Watch with Me One Hour?"

The most impressive story about watching is also Jesus' hardest hour, the night in Gethsemane. The heading in Luther's Bible is "The Struggle in Gethsemane," for this is Jesus' inner struggle with godforsakenness. His prayer to the God he calls Abba, dear Father, is not answered. The cup of eternal death does not pass him by. The night of what Martin Buber called "the eclipse of God" falls on him and on those who are his, and on this world. This eclipse of God corresponds with what mystics call "the dark night of the soul," where you lose all orientation and all your feelings for life dry up. That is why in this hour Christ began "to be greatly distressed and troubled," says Mark, "to be sorrowful and troubled," writes Matthew. "My soul is very sorrowful, even to death," he tells the disciples. Earlier he had often withdrawn and prayed all night long by himself in the hills. But in this hour he is afraid of being alone with his God, and he begs his disciples: "Stay here and watch." Jesus prays, and struggles with the dark and mysterious will of his God, and his disciples are supposed to take over the watching that belongs to prayer. But no, Jesus enters this eclipse of God by praying and watching: "Not my will, but your will be done." Yet his disciples fall into a deep, oblivious sleep: "Simon Peter, are you asleep? Could you not watch with me one hour?" This scene, so saddening for Jesus and so shaming for the disciples, is repeated three times. Jesus wrestles with the dark side of God, and the stifling unconsciousness of sleep descends on the disciples until the night has passed and the day of Golgotha has begun, into which Jesus goes actively and resolutely: "Get up, let us be going. My betrayer is at hand." We all know what happens after that. But what strange kind of sleep was it that overcame the truest of the true?

In the monastery of San Croce in Florence, there is a remarkable fresco in one of the cells, painted by Fra Angelico. It is of the scene in Gethsemane. Jesus is praying, the disciples are sleeping, but two people are watching at Jesus' side—two women. The one looks wide-eyed in the direction of Jesus as he prays. The other is reading the Bible. These women are Martha and Mary. They are watching with Jesus, and over him, in the hour of his god-forsakenness, just as the women watched from afar when Jesus was crucified and the male disciples had fled away.

Why do the disciples fall asleep? If the Master whom they have followed without fear and trembling begins to tremble and fear himself, some cruel and inscrutable danger must surely be lurking. What danger? Through his healings of the sick, Jesus had communicated the nearness of God in ways that could be seen and felt—through the senses. But for the disciples, this nearness now evidently turns into God's absence. Their feeling that God had found them is turned upside down. It becomes a sense of being lost without anything to which to cling. It is as if they have been felled by some blow. Their reaction is numbness and the sleep of hopelessness. We know what this is like. Impending danger can stimulate us, but danger with no way out numbs us, and we take flight into sleep, a sleep which protects us from what is unendurable. It is not a natural, refreshing sleep. It is the petrifying of all our senses, which makes us sick. Our eyes are open, but we no longer see anything. Our ears are open, but we are deaf and hear nothing. We are apathetic, and feel nothing.

Spiritual Paralyses Today

The paralyzing sleep that fell on Jesus' disciples in Gethsemane was not their problem only. It is our problem too. How do we react to unknown dangers?

For millions of years, our consciousness has learned to react to the most widely differing dangers in life-supporting ways. How? Through fear, which keeps us wakeful and all our senses keyed up, so that we can counter whatever threatens us. In our civilized societies there are in-built securities for our survival, from lightning conductors to dikes against storm tides.

But today there are dangers that are present without our perceiving them. In 1986, in the catastrophe in the Chernobyl nuclear power station, deadly radioactivity was released that people could neither smell nor taste nor see. It contaminated huge stretches of land, and up to now has cost the lives of 150,000 people. In such nuclear dangers our senses let us down. Our highly developed danger antennae do not react to these perils. "Our nuclear power stations are completely safe," we are told, year after year. But no insurance company is prepared to insure a nuclear power plant against a meltdown, because human beings are not secure.

The way we react to the growing ecological crisis is no different. We do not perceive the destruction of the ozone layer with the help of our senses. It does not touch us directly. The connection between the increase in ultraviolet rays and skin cancer has been proved, but only statistically, so no one needs to feel personally concerned.

The time that elapses between cause and effect is too long for us to perceive it directly, so ecological crises leave us relatively cold. We suppress our knowledge of them because "we don't want to know"; we don't want to know about the damage we are inflicting today on the already damaged world our children and grandchildren are going to live in. This is "ecological numbing."

Growing climatic changes are much more threatening than we have assumed up to now. According to the Third Report of the International Panel of Climate Change 2001, global warming must definitely be blamed on human activity. In the next forty years, temperatures are going to rise by 2 to 5°C. Ocean levels will rise, river estuaries will be flooded, many islands in the Pacific will disappear, and there will continually be "natural" catastrophes that are in fact man-made. In the year 2050 there will be about 150 million climate refugees. But our "way of life" must be preserved, and, as we know, this way of life is characterized by its extensive use of energy and even more extensive atmospheric pollution. Our eyes are open but we do not see; our ears are open but we do not hear—until catastrophe overtakes us. And then we will swear that this is all new to us.

We are no longer aware of true reality. We live only in our own dreams, and think that our illusions of reality are reality itself. We are asleep in the agreeable dreams of our fantasy worlds.

What is especially seductive and fascinating in these wishful worlds of ours is our own image of ourselves. We see ourselves as we would like to be. It is like the fairy tale, "Mirror, mirror on the wall." It is always supposed to tell us that we are "the fairest one of all"—or the strongest, or the most clever, or whatever we like best. We must learn to see ourselves in the mirror of other people's eyes, and especially the eyes of the victims. That is painful, and hurts the image of ourselves we cherish so much, but it helps us to wake up from our dreams and to come face to face with reality.

Watch and Pray

My old Bible dictionary tells me that "watching discerns the danger—praying brings help from God." That is true, but which comes first? First watching then praying, or first praying then waking up and watching?

What are we seeking when we pray? When we pray, we are seeking the reality of God and are breaking out of the hall of mirrors of our own wishes and illusions in which we are imprisoned. This means we wake up out of the petrifications and numbness of our feelings. If in prayer we seek the reality of God's world—remember the first line of the Lord's Prayer: "Hallowed be thy name, thy kingdom . . ."—then that is the exact opposite of "the opium of the people." Prayer is more like the beginning of a cure for the numbing addictions of the secular world.

In prayer we wake up to the world as it is spread out before God in all its heights and depths. We perceive the sighing of our fellow creatures and hear the cries of the created beings that have fallen dumb. We hear the song of praise of the blossoming spring, and chime in with it. We feel the divine love for life that allows pain to touch us to the quick and kindles joy. Real prayer to God awakens all our senses and alerts our minds and spirits. The person who prays, lives more attentively.

Pray watchfully. That is only possible if we do not pray mystically with closed eyes, but instead pray messianically, with eyes open for God's future in the world. Christian faith is not blind faith. It is the wakeful expectation of

God, which touches all our senses. The early Christians prayed standing, looking up, with outstretched arms and wide-open eyes, ready to walk or to leap forward. We can see this from the pictures in the catacombs in Rome. Their posture reflects tense expectation, not quiet heart searching. We do not watch just because of the dangers that threaten us. We are expecting the salvation of the world. We are watching for God's advent. With tense attention, we open all our senses for the coming of God into our lives, into our society, to this earth.

Watch prayerfully. The ancient wisdom of the masters of prayer and mediation is that it is good to pray in the morning, at the dawn of the day, in the hour between sleeping and waking, and to rejoice in the reality of God and his world.

Concentrating, praying, waking up, watching and praying—all this reveals to our lives the daybreak colors of the future, and it leads to the call of Jesus who, having watched and prayed in Gethsemane, called to his sleeping disciples: "Get up, let us be going." Let us wake up and see what God will bring on this new day.

"Keep awake and be sober" (1 Thess. 5:6). This is the next thing we hear. If what we want is to be full of enthusiasm, this brings us down to earth. The people who are sober are the ones who are not drunk and so do not suffer from hallucinations and who do not let themselves be deluded by illusions, either pious or secular. When sobriety is added to the wakefulness that comes from praying, we will not fool ourselves, and will not let ourselves be fooled either. We will see reality as it is, and expose ourselves to it in its workaday guise as well as in its surprises. Then we will discover that reality is far more fantastic than our best fantasies. But we will perceive too that the pain which reality imposes on us is better than the self-immunizations with which we try to protect ourselves but through which we in fact wall ourselves in.

In German the word for "sober" can also mean "empty" —an empty stomach. People who are "sober" in this sense have not yet eaten anything; they begin the day fasting. They are hungry. In a transferred sense we call realists "sober." They see reality as it is. If we are sober in this sense, we are hungry for reality, for God is in the reality; and then we forget the thousand possibilities we dream on. One single experienced reality is richer than a thousand conceived-of possibilities. This is why contact with reality is so important.

Watch and expect. When we wake up in the morning we expect the new day. In the same way, the waking that springs from prayer to God also leads to the expectation of God in the life we experience. I wake up and open all my senses for life and for death, for the fulfillments and also for the disappointments, for what is painful as well as for what gives joy. I expect the presence of God in everything I meet and everything I do. God's history with me, and with us, goes on. There is nothing more exhilarating than to experience one's life-history with God in full awareness by asking, What has God in mind for me? What does God expect of me? What is God saying to me through the things that are happening in the world?

Watch and see. Remarkably enough, watching and praying have not so much to do with faith, but everything with seeing: "The LORD opens the eyes of the blind" (Ps. 146:8). Israel's Wisdom tells us, "The hearing ear and the seeing eye—the LORD has made them both" (Prov. 20:12), but it is by no means a matter of course that people who have eyes can also see, and that people with ears can hear. "Seeing they do not perceive," complains Jesus, according to Matthew 13:13, and "hearing they do not listen, nor do they understand." He is referring to the presence of the kingdom of God among us. But he means his presence among us today too: "I was hungry and you gave me no food, I was thirsty and you gave me nothing to drink, I was a stranger and you did not welcome me. . . . Then they will answer, 'Lord, when was it that we saw you hungry or thirsty or a stranger . . . ?' Then he will answer them, 'Truly I tell you, just as you did not do it to one of the least of these, you did not do it to me'" (Matt. 25:42–45). That is the great judgment pronounced on us.

How do we learn to have seeing eyes for Christ's presence among us? Where are our eyes opened? Archbishop Oscar Arnulfo Romero was a faithful, conservative churchman. When he was fifty-nine years old he had a conversion experience. "He discovered in the poor the way of faith in God," writes Jon Sobrino in his book *Oscar Romero: Memories in Mosaic.* "In all the crucified men and women of history, the crucified God became present to him. . . . In the faces of the poor he saw the distorted face of God." Romero put himself on their side, and a short time afterward was shot in front of the altar while saying mass in San Salvador.

Where was God when the mass murders took place at the World Trade Center on September 11, 2001? If we were to ask why God permitted this catastrophe, would we answer like some well-known fundamentalist preachers— that it was because he wanted to punish secular, liberal, or homosexual America? But wouldn't that mean that our God is the God of terrorists, and that the terrorists were the servants who carried out his orders? Ought we not rather ask where God was in those mass murders, and look for his presence among the victims? Doesn't God weep over the death of so many of his beloved children? Jesus wept over the coming destruction of Jerusalem (Luke

19:41). Tears ran down the face of the suffering God at Ground Zero, and people who believe in God for Christ's sake are called to "stand beside God in his suffering," as Dietrich Bonhoeffer wrote during the resistance to the Nazi murderers.

Watch and perceive. To go through life with eyes open for God, to see Christ in oppressed and unimportant people—that is what praying and watching is all about. We believe so that we can see, not so that we can shut our eyes to the world. We believe so that we can see—and can endure what we see.

To sum up what watching and praying is about, we would have to say that it is about an attentive life. Goodwill and helpfulness are fine, but they are not enough. Attentiveness is necessary, so that we do the right thing at the right time in the right place.

"Watchman, What of the Night?"

Darkness and night are always symbols for the godforsakenness of the world and for the lostness of men and women. In the darkness and in the night we see nothing, and the best thing is to sleep until day. There is an apt passage in Isaiah: In exile and far from home, strangers among strangers, the Israelite prisoners come to the prophet and ask, "Watchman, what of the night?" He replies, "Morning comes, and also the night. If you will inquire, inquire; come back again" (Isa. 21:12). But Paul, Christ's witness, proclaims, "The night is far gone, the day is near. Let us then lay aside the works of darkness and put on the armor of light" (Rom. 13:12). So it is "time to get up from sleep" and to live life in the light of God's new day.

In these daybreak colors of Christ's day, we will pray and watch, watch and be sober, watch and expect God, see and perceive Christ in our minds, and learn to live attentively in God's Spirit, wholly present with all our senses and all our powers.

In our dreams, each of us is alone, but when we wake up we are in a world we share with others. As Heraclitus said, "The wakeful share a world, whereas every sleeper turns to the world that is his alone." The wakeful perceive and know each other in the world they share.

"Get up," says Christ to us benumbed disciples, "and let us be going."

Chapter 5

The Crucified God Yesterday and Today: 1972–2002

Jürgen Moltmann

Translated by Margaret Kohl

*T*he Crucified God, first published in Germany in 1972, "is undoubtedly one of the theological classics of the second half of the twentieth century," wrote Richard Bauckham in his preface to the SCM Classics edition (London 2001). "What marks it as a classic is, that when one rereads it several decades later, themes, which were innovative in its time, seem now rather familiar . . . but also that it still shocks and surprises, enlightens and provokes, with its dialectical sharpness of expression. . . . It is a passionate book, written 'so to speak with my lifeblood,' as Moltmann said of it much later" (p. ix).

I am not sure whether Richard Bauckham is right, but I am certain this book was part of my personal "wrestling with God," my suffering under the dark side of God, the hidden face of God, the *hester panim*, as the Jews say, the godforsakenness of the victims and the godlessness of the guilty in the human history of violence and suffering.

In July 1943 at the age of seventeen, I lay watching bombs rain down all around me in my hometown of Hamburg. Forty thousand people, including women and children, were killed as a result of that bombing or burned in the firestorm that followed. Miraculously I survived. To this day I do not know why I am not dead like my comrades. My question in that inferno was not, "Why is God letting this happen?" but rather, "Where is God?" Is God far away from us, absent, in his heaven? Or is God among us, suffering with us? Does God share in our suffering?

Two questions occur to me at this point. One is the theoretical question about accusing God in the face of the pain of the victims—this is the so-called theodicy question. The other is the existential question about community with God in suffering. The first question presupposes an apathetic, untouchable God in heaven, while the second question is searching for a compassionate God, "the fellow-sufferer who understands us" (Alfred North Whitehead).

Yes, I remember the catastrophe of my people, the inexorable crime against the Jewish people that has the name of shame, "Auschwitz." I shall never forget the pictures of the dead in the concentration camp of Bergen-Belsen shown to us POWs in England in October 1945. It was so unbelievable, but it was true; the crimes were committed in the name of my people. I shall never forget walking through the remnants and ruins of the death camp of Maidanek, near Lublin, in November 1961. I would have rather sunk to the ground than gone on, and there, all of a sudden, I became certain that these murdered people would live. The horrors over the crimes of the Holocaust had weighed on me and many other people of my generation in Germany ever since the end of the war. Much time passed before we could emerge from the silence that stops the mouths of people over whom the clouds of the victims hang heavy. Did God let this happen? Where is

God? Is God far away from the victims of violence, or is God on their side, crying and suffering with them? My book *The Crucified God* was said to be a Christian theology "after Auschwitz." This is true. It was for me an attempt to speak to God, to trust in God and speak about God in the shadows of Auschwitz and in view of the victims of my people. The God-question has been identical with the cry of the victims for justice and the hunger of the perpetrators for a way back from the path of death.

The Crucified God is in essence a book about believing in God after the cross of Christ. What we can say about God "after Auschwitz" depends on what we can say about God after the crucifixion of Christ, hearing the dying Jesus' cry of abandonment: "My God, why have you forsaken me?" The whole book can be understood as a theological interpretation of these words from the Gospels of Mark and Matthew.

I remember April 6, 1968. I was participating in an international "Theology of Hope" conference at Duke University when Harvey Cox stormed into the hall and cried, "Martin Luther King has been shot!" The conference ended immediately and the participants returned home because many cities in America were burning that night. I left a few days later for Tübingen, and I promised my American friends that whenever I returned to their country, I would not speak about the theology of hope any more but of the cross: "In a civilization that glorifies success and happiness and is blind for the suffering of others, people's eyes may be opened to the truth, if they remember that at the centre of the Christian Faith stands the assailed, tormented Christ, dying in forsakenness. The recollection that God raised the Crucified one and made him the 'Hope of the world' must lead churches to break their alliances with the violent and enter into solidarity with the humiliated." I wrote this in 1970, two years before *The Crucified God*.

And where are we today? Before September 11, 2001, America was successfully globalizing American power and culture with a kind of universal optimism in the New World Order, or *novus ordo seclorum*, as it is written on every dollar bill. After the terrorist attacks on the World Trade Center and the Pentagon, a new "age of anxiety" seems to have come over us. In order not to sink into an abyss of despair, we should discover anew the face of the crucified One in the faces of the victims of violence, the "crucified people," as Jon Sobrino would say. What is the crucial theological question? Should we ask, "Why did God let this massacre happen?" Would this not say that our God is the God of the terrorists, and that they were unconsciously God's obedient servants? Or should we ask, "Where was God in these attacks?" and find God as the suffering God among the victims? Is God not weeping and crying over the death of his beloved children? Jesus wept over the destruction of Jerusalem (Luke 19:41), and so tears rolled down the face of God at Ground Zero as surely as they did over Jerusalem, and we are called to participate in these sufferings of God with all our compassion.

This was and is the decisive question of *The Crucified God*. Is God the transcendent and untouched stage manager of the theater of this violent world, or is God in Christ the central engaged figure of the world tragedy?

In the next section, I will explain the basic themes of *The Crucified God*. Then I will summarize the criticism of Karl Rahner, Johann Baptist Metz, Hans Küng, Dorothee Sölle, and feminist theology. To conclude, I will look into the future of the risen Christ and the coming joy of God.

Basic Themes of *The Crucified God*

Is God Passible or Impassible?

Is God capable of suffering? If we follow the fashion of Greek philosophy and ask what attributes are "appropriate" to God (Gr.: *theoprepes*), differentiation, diversity, movement, and suffering all have to be excluded from the divine nature. The divine nature is incapable of suffering; otherwise it would not be divine. The absolute subject of modern metaphysics is also incapable of suffering; otherwise it would not be absolute. Impassible, immovable, uncompounded, and self-sufficing, the Deity stands over against a moved, divided, suffering, and never self-sufficient world. The divine substance is the founder and sustainer of this world of transitory phenomena. It abides eternally, and so it cannot be subjected to this world's destiny. This is called the metaphysical apathy axiom. We find it in Aristotle's *Metaphysics*, book 12.

If we turn instead to the theological proclamation of the Christian tradition, we find at its center the passion of Christ. The gospel tells us about the suffering of Christ for the redemption of the world; the Eucharist communicates the self-giving of Christ in the form of bread and wine. When Christ's Passion is made present to us in word and sacrament, faith is awakened in us—the Christian faith in God, not just a certain monotheistic belief. We believe in God for Christ's sake because God himself is involved in Christ's passion story. But in what way? If the Deity cannot suffer, how can we see Christ's passion as the revelation of God? Does God let Christ suffer for/with us, or does God himself suffer for/with us in Christ?

The ability to identify God with the suffering Christ dwindles in proportion to the importance given to the apathy axiom in the doctrine of God. If God is incapable of suffering, then Christ's passion can only be viewed as a human tragedy, and there is no redeeming power in his passion. If we want to say both, we end up formulating paradoxes, as did Bertrand Brasnett in his book *The Suffering of the Impassible God*.[1] I think it would be more consistent if we simply stop making the metaphysical axiom of God's apathy our starting point in theology and start from the biblical axiom of God's passion instead, so as to understand Christ's suffering as the *passion of the passionate God*. The word *passion* has the double meaning of suffering and overwhelming feeling and ardor, and the God of Israel is a God full of passion for the life of his people and for justice on his earth.

Why did patristic theology hold fast to the apathy axiom (with the exception of Origen), although Christian devotion adored at the same time the crucified Christ as God? We can see two reasons:

1. God's essential impassibility distinguishes the Deity from human beings, who are subject to suffering, transience, and death.
2. Salvation is the deification of human beings by giving them a share in eternal life. If we become immortal, we shall also become impassible: Apathy is divine nature and the fulfillment of human salvation in eternal life.

Logically these arguments fall short because they take only into account a single alternative: either essential incapacity of suffering or fateful subjection to suffering. But there is a third form of suffering, *active suffering*, which involves the willingness to open oneself to be touched, moved, affected by others—and that means the suffering of *passionate love*. If God were in every respect incapable of suffering, God would also be incapable of love. If God is love, however, God opens God's self for the suffering that love for others brings. God does not suffer, as we do, out of deficiency of being, but God does suffer from love for creation, which is the overflowing superabundance of God's divine being. In this sense, God can suffer, will suffer, and is suffering in the world.

For Whom Did Christ Die?

The traditional answer to this question is that Christ died for sinners. In *The Crucified God* I expanded the question of salvation from the traditional concern with sin to encompass also the contemporary concern with innocent and meaningless suffering. Those with whom Christ is identified in his abandonment and death are the godless on the one hand, and the godforsaken on the other, or, more concretely, the evildoers and their victims. Traditional doctrines of justification are sin-oriented; modern liberation theology is victim-oriented. Both sides belong together in a world of sin and suffering, violence and victims.

Why did God take the suffering of Christ onto God's self? The first answer is: To be present and beside us in our suffering and abandonment. This leads to a *solidarity Christology:* Christ our divine brother "emptied himself, taking the form of a slave . . . humbled himself and became obedient to the point of death—even death on a cross" (Phil. 2:7–8). If God takes this road with Christ and God is where Christ is, then Christ brings God's fellowship to people, who are as humiliated and emptied of their identity as Christ was. Christ's cross stands between the countless crosses that line the paths of the powerful and violent, from Spartacus to the concentration camps and the "disappeared" in Latin American dictatorships. His cross stands between our crosses as a sign that God participates in our sufferings. This was the comforting insight of Dietrich Bonhoeffer in the Gestapo cell: "Only the suffering God can help" (*Letters and Papers from Prison*). This was the conversion experience of Archbishop Oscar Arnulfo Romero in San Salvador, as described by Jon Sobrino: "In the crucified people of history the crucified God became present to him. In the eyes of the poor and oppressed of his people he saw the disfigured face of God." Christ took upon himself humiliation and passion so that he could become the brother of the humiliated and forsaken and bring them God's embracing presence.

> And when the human hearts are breaking
> 　　Under sorrow's iron rod,
> Then there is the selfsame aching
> 　　Deep within the heart of God.[2]

The second answer leads to *reconciliation Christology*. From very early on, Christians saw Christ's passion as the vicarious divine suffering for the reconciliation of sinners. Following the model of the Suffering Servant in Isaiah 53, they saw Christ as the divine son who reconciles sinners with God through his vicarious suffering. Is this necessary? How does it work? Without forgiveness of sin, the guilty cannot live, for they have lost all their self-identity and consequently also their self-respect. But there is no forgiveness without atonement. Yet atonement is not possible for human beings because the wrong that has been done cannot be made undone or made good by any human act. Only God can reconcile guilty people with their past. How? The Suffering Servant of Isaiah takes away the sins of the people by "carrying the people's sin." By carrying and bearing human sin, God transforms their aggressions into his suffering.

Christ is the brother of the victims and the redeemer of the guilty. He "carries" on the one hand "the sufferings of the world" and on the other hand "the sins of the world."

Both sides of Christ belong together for the redemption of the world, but they are not equal. Victims have a long memory, for the traces of suffering are deeply etched into their souls and often into their bodies too. People who have committed the injury always have short memories. They do not know what they have done because they do not want to know. They are dependent on the memory of the victims if they want to see who they are and be reconciled. They must learn to see themselves with the eyes of their victims.

Reconciliation is not an individualistic act between "me and my God" but a communal act between God, the perpetrators, and the victims.

When I wrote *The Crucified God*, I turned the traditional question upside down. The question traditionally asked is the soteriological question: What does the cross of Christ mean for our redemption? My question was the theological one: What does the cross of Christ mean for God himself? I came face to face with the pain of God the Father of Christ, who suffered with him. If Christ dies with the cry of being forsaken by God, then in God the Father there must be a correspondingly profound experience of his forsakenness by his beloved Son. In 2002 Peter Dudeney from Boston wrote to me: "I remember while reading *The Crucified God* being struck by the realization that Jesus experienced ultimate abandonment and the Father ultimate bereavement and that no one, in whatever extremity, will ever, can ever, be beyond the fellowship of God and the power of the Spirit."

The suffering of the Father is different from the suffering of the Son. The Son experienced dying in forsakenness, while the Father experienced the death of the Son. We can illustrate this with our own experiences. At my end I shall experience dying, but not my own death, while in those I love, I experience death when they die because I have to survive their death. The death of Christ reaches deep into the nature of God, and, above all other meanings, is an event that takes place in the innermost nature of God, the Trinity: Do we see at Golgotha a fatherless Son and a son-less Father? "One of the Trinity suffered," said the early church theologian Cyril, and this so-called 'theopaschitic principle' is now accepted. I would like to add that where one suffers, the others suffer too. Christ's death on the cross is an intratrinitarian event before it assumes significance for the redemption of the world. There is a famous medieval image of the Trinity, the so-called mercy seat or chair of grace, sometimes called even "the pain of God." With an expression of intensive pain God the Father carries in his hands the crossbeam of the cross on which the dead Son hangs, while the Spirit in the form of a dove descends from the face of the Father to the face of the Son. This is an image of the Trinity with the cross at the center. What we are shown is the breathtaking scene of Holy Saturday, after the death of the Son on Good Friday and before his raising from the dead on Easter Sunday. There is a mystical moment of silence between cross and resurrection.

It follows from this that a true theology of the cross (Luther) must be a Trinitarian theology (beyond Luther). The Trinity is the theological background for what really took place on Golgotha between Christ and the God whom he called in Gethsemane "Abba, my dear father." On the other hand, the crucified Christ is the revelation of the Trinitarian mystery of God. Only when we plumb the depths of this pain of God can we grasp the immeasurable Easter jubilation of the joy of God and of the whole creation.

Consent

The Crucified God became controversial in the best sense of the word. It stimulated people to think about suffering and the crucified Christ for themselves. I received strong support from Anglican theologians such as Kenneth Woolcombe and Richard Bauckham, from liberation theologians such as Jon Sobrino and Leonardo Boff, from the Korean Minjung theologian Ahn Byun-Mu, and, to my surprise, also from the Orthodox Romanian theologian Dumitru Staniloae, who found the pain of God included in the concept of the merciful God. Many authors followed me with titles such as *The God of Weakness* (John Timmer), *The Suffering God* (Charles Ohlrich), *The Passion of God* (W. McWilliams), *God and Human Suffering* (Douglas John Hall), *The Disabled God* (Nancy Eiesland), *La Croix de Dieu* (Jean-Louis Souletie), to mention only a few. Numerous dissertations were written on the topic. But what impressed me most were the many personal letters from people in prisons, hospitals, and basic communities in slums, people who have to live in the "shadows of the cross," or in the "dark night of the soul," or among the crucified people of this world. People are still coming to me after thirty years, speaking about the personal consolation they found in this book. When they cried out to God, they found the suffering God at their side.

In 1990, I received a letter from Robert McAfee Brown. He told me a moving story from San Salvador. On November 16, 1989, six well-known Jesuits, together with their housekeeper and her daughter, were brutally murdered in the university there by a group of soldiers. The rector of the university, Father Ignacio Ellacuria, was one of them. Jon Sobrino escaped the massacre only because he happened not to be in the country at the time. The letter continues: "When the killers were dragging some of the bodies back into the building, as they took the body of Ramon Moreno into John's room, they hit a bookcase and knocked a book on the floor, which became drenched with the martyr's blood. In the morning when they picked up the book, they found that it was *The Crucified God*." Two years later I made a pilgrimage to the graves of the martyrs and found my book, *Il Dio Crucificado*, there under glass, as a sign and symbol of what really happened in this place. It gave me a great deal to think about.

Critique

God Cannot Suffer!

In his last interview, Karl Rahner answered the question of whether or not God suffers rather roughly:

> I would say that there is a modern tendency to develop a theology of the death of God, that, in the last analysis, seems to me to be gnostic. One can find this in Hans Urs von Balthasar and in Adrienne von Speyr, it also appears in an independent form in Moltmann. To put it crudely: It does not help me to escape from my mess and mix-up and despair [German: *mein Dreck und Schlamassel und meiner Verzweiflung*] if God is in the same predicament [German: *Wenn es Gott genau so dreckig geht*]. It is for me a part of my consolation, to realize that God, when and insofar as he entered into this history as his own, did it in a different way than I did. From the beginning I am cemented into this horribleness [German:

Gräßlichkeit], while God is in a true and authentic and consoling sense the God who cannot suffer, "Deus impassibilis, and immutable God, Deus immutabilis." In Moltmann and others I sense a theology of absolute paradox of Patripassianism, and to this I would say: What use would that be to me as consolation in the true sense of the word?[3]

I found these statements of Karl Rahner only after his death. So I answered in a kind of posthumous letter. Here are a few excerpts:

I am disturbed by your objection that God "in a consoling sense is the God who cannot suffer." I find no connection between consolation and apathy. . . . Of course God entered into our history of suffering in a different way, he was not subjected to it against his will. That God does not suffer as finite creatures do does not mean that he is incapable of suffering in any way. God is capable of suffering because he is capable of love. His very being is mercy. . . . I cannot imagine an impassible God as a God who consoles in a personal sense. He seems to me to be as cold and hard and unfeeling as cement. . . . What disturbed and shocked me, though, was what you said about yourself: "From the beginning I am cemented into its horribleness." That sounds bitter, cut off, isolated and incapable of movement . . . like a life which is unloved and incapable of love. And: With what right do we human beings say that God is "incapable"? Do we not "cement" God in with the negations of this negative theology? If that is the case, then a personal experience of being locked in and a divine image of a *Deus impassibilis* go closely together. How can a

God who is locked into his immobility and impassibility become a comfort for the person whose situation also seems to be like that? In that case God would indeed be in the same predicament, and neither God nor human beings could find comfort in eternity.[4]

Johann Baptist Metz followed the argument of his master, Karl Rahner, and added that God must not suffer because the theodicy question—If there is a God, why is there evil and suffering?—must be kept open. At the end we shall accuse God and ask: Why has there been so much evil and suffering in the world? And then God must answer us. A God who has been present in our suffering and who took up his cross for us could not be accused. Metz cannot find the christological answer to his open theodicy question. There is a christological deficit in his fundamental theology.

It is similiar with Hans Küng. God is for him—as for Ignatius—*Deus semper major*, the always greater God. In the face of innocent suffering there remains only a "theology of silence." When Aaron's sons were killed by God's fire, the biblical statement is short: "And Aaron kept silent." Küng wants to find the consent of Jews and Muslims. His doctrine of God is therefore without Christ. He is looking for a common belief in the God of Jews, Christians, and Muslims, for a monotheistic world movement. This, however, must not deny that Christians believe in God for Christ's sake.

Did God Kill His Own Son?

The most severe attack on my theology of the cross came unexpectedly from Dorothee Sölle, at that time more a liberal theologian than a feminist, in her book *Suffering*.[5]

MFHD

Yes

In my interpretation of the godforsakenness of Christ on the cross she saw signs of a "theological sadism." For me, Christ's godforsakenness was the most profound expression of his solidarity with forsaken men and women. Dorothee, however, read the passion story morally and rose up in arms against such a "sadistic God" who abandons and sacrifices his "own son." She even compared this God with Heinrich Himmler. This viewpoint was so alien to me that I had not even considered it. But ever since then, the legend has gone around that, in Moltmann's view, "God killed his own son" on Golgotha.

Feminist theologians in Germany and the United States willingly picked up this moral criticism of the theology of the cross as specific "feminist critique" without realizing that this is old Enlightenment criticism against atonement theology, the sacrifice in Roman Catholic mass, and sacrificial morality. More recently this criticism has appeared in the reproach of victimization in patriarchal religions and has been justified by the defamation of the Christian theology of the cross. The "sadistic God" is now turned into a heavenly practitioner of child-abuse (as Moloch of the Phoenicians), on the pattern of the atrocious fathers who abuse their own daughters. I am absolutely against the victimization of sons and daughters, because I myself hardly survived being "sacrificed" for my "holy fatherland" in World War II. As a matter of fact, the Christian theology of the cross of Christ ended sacrificial religions "once for all," just as the Mount Moriah story of Isaac's nonsacrifice stopped child sacrifices as religious requirement (cf. again Moloch, the child-eater, or Kali, the boy-eating goddess of Calcutta). Dorothee Sölle and some German feminist theologians have turned more and more to the recognition of the presence of the suffering God in the pains and sorrows of suffering people.

The Crucified God Tomorrow

I started my theological writing with *The Theology of Hope*. This was an interpretation of the resurrected Christ and Easter. The second book was *The Crucified God*, and this was an interpretation of Golgotha and Good Friday. At this point, I decided to balance the two books with a study of the Holy Spirit and an interpretation of Pentecost, so *The Church in the Power of the Spirit* followed in 1975. After establishing this foundation for my theology, I was ready for more systematic books. I wrote my systematic contributions to theology from 1980 to 1999. The secret goal that I was searching for all the time was a theological reflection of the Easter joy and a theological anticipation of the eternal glory in the new creation of all things. The depth of the cross and the height of the resurrection of Christ are not in balance. "How much more . . . ," the apostle Paul always said (Gr: *pollo malon*). "Christ Jesus, who died, yes, who was raised, . . ." (Rom. 8:34). "But where sin increased, grace abounded all the more" (Rom. 5:20). There is a surplus value of the victory over the defeat, of the resurrection over the crucifixion, of grace over sin and joy over pain. Good Friday is at the center of this world, but Easter morning is the sunrise of the coming of God and the morning of the new life and is the beginning of the future of this world. I love the Orthodox Easter liturgy with the hymn:

> Now all is filled with light,
> heaven and earth and the realm of the dead.
> The whole creation rejoices in Christ's resurrection,
> which is the true foundation. . . .
> Let us embrace one another.

Let us speak to those who hate us:
For the resurrection's sake we will forgive one
Another everything. And so let us cry:
Christ is risen from the dead.

I finally found this theology of joy and jubilation in my book on eschatology, *The Coming of God: Christian Eschatology*, in which I do not deal with "the end of the world" and those who may be "left behind," but with the coming of God. I say in the last sentences: "The feast of eternal joy is prepared by the fulness of God and the rejoicing of all created being. . . . The laughter of the universe is God's delight. It is the universal Easter laughter" in heaven and on earth.[6] This is the promise and the future of the crucified God.

Notes

1. Bertrand Brasnett, *The Suffering of the Impassible God* (London: SPCK, 1928).
2. T. Rees in *Hymns and Psalms* (London: Methodist Publishing House, 1983), no. 36, stanza 2.
3. Paul Imhoff and Hubert Biallowons, eds., *Im Gespräch/Karl Rahner* (Munich: Kösel Verlag, 1982), 245.
4. Jürgen Moltmann, *History and the Triune God: Contributions to Trinitarian Theology*, trans. John Bowden (New York: Crossroad, 1992), 122–24.
5. Dorothee Sölle, *Suffering*, trans. Everett R. Kalin (Philadelphia: Fortress Press, 1984).
6. Jürgen Moltmann, *The Coming of God: Christian Eschatology*, trans. Margaret Kohl (Minneapolis: Fortress Press, 1996), 338–39.

Chapter 6

Globalization, Terrorism, and the Beginning of Life

Jürgen Moltmann

The Beginning of Life: Christian Hope

If we ask whether our world has an end, we are asking a typically apocalyptic question. Some people talk about "the end of all things," others about "the end of the world," or "the end of history." Why do we ask about the end at all? Can't we endure the state of things as they are any longer? Have we had enough of this world? Or do we fear for the continued existence of things we love and cherish? Can't we get enough of this world? Can something be good only if it ends in a good way? Or is an end with terror better than this terror without end? Every thought about "the end" is ambivalent. It can fascinate us, but it can terrify us too.

In Christian theology, questions about "the end" are treated in eschatology under the heading of "the final questions." Eschatology is the study of "the last things" (Gr.: *ta eschata*). The end will bring "the final solution" of all unsolved problems in personal life, in human history, and in the cosmos. Apocalyptic imagination has always painted with tremendous passion God's great final judgment in the world's last day. The good will go to heaven, the wicked to hell, and the earth will be annihilated in a holocaust of fire. We know too the apocalyptic images of the final battle between God and the devil, Christ and antichrist, the good and the evil in "the valley of Armageddon."

All these ideas and images are certainly soundly apocalyptic, but are they Christian? The authentic Christian expectation of the future has nothing at all to do with final solutions of this kind, for its focus is not *the end*—the end of life, the end of history, or the end of the world. It is rather *the beginning*—the beginning of true life, the beginning of the kingdom of God, and the beginning of the new creation of all things. When Dietrich Bonhoeffer was taken away to the place of execution in Flossenbürg concentration camp on April 9, 1945, he took leave of his fellow prisoners with these words: "This is the end—for me the beginning of life." One is reminded of T. S. Eliot's "East Coker": "In the end is my beginning."

Expectations of the end are only Christian if they conceive their future horizons out of the remembrance of Christ's death on the cross and the resurrection of the crucified Christ with the dead into the eternal life of the coming glory of God. For Christ's end too was, and is, after all, his true beginning. Christian hope of the future does not prolong or extrapolate into the future the lines of the past and the present of world history, so as to postulate a good end or, more generally, a bad one. Instead it perceives in the cross of Christ the anticipation of the end of this world of sin, death, and evil, because—yes, because— in Christ's resurrection it recognizes the deliverance from evil in the beginning of the new life and the new creation of all things. In the energies of the Spirit of Christ it already experiences that new beginning here and now, being reborn to a living hope.

How does this work? Nobody can be perfect, but everyone must be able to start anew. All that matters in life and death is the new beginning. If a child falls down, the child learns to stand up again. Failures and disappointments are no problems. It is important to stand up and try it again. Christian faith is in essence resurrection belief. This is grounded in Christ's resurrection from the dead and opens the expectation to eternal life, and it is the present power to find the beginning of new and true life here and now. Christians are by grace beginners of life. Their freedom is the ability to begin life afresh because God's grace is new every morning. In our lifetime we may see only the beginnings and the first steps, but we trust that God sees the perfection. "I am confident," wrote Paul to the Philippians (1:6), "the one who began a good work among you will bring it to completion by the day of Jesus Christ." And no death can hinder God to do this!

How are the end and the beginning, beginning and end, related to each other? Radical social critics in Germany liked to quote the dictum of the philosopher Theodor W. Adorno of the Frankfurt school: "There is no true life in the life which is false." This seems to be self-evident. But for the Christian hope, Christ, who has come into this false world, is the real beginning of true life in the very midst of this false life. This is why we feel in Christian hope with the beginning of the new life the end of the false life too. In light of the resurrected Christ we perceive "the world under the cross" and see the world with the eyes of the dying Christ with everything that is false in it, everything that terrorizes and destroys. This is what is to be brought to an end and must disappear. Hope in the resurrection of life leads us to the realism of the cross.

It is, however, not the end of the world that brings a new creation. The very opposite is true. It is only God's new beginning that brings this perverted world to its deserved end. We first perceive the darkness of the night in the light of the new day, we recognize evil only in the light of the good, and we feel the deadliness of death only through our love for life. The annihilation of life, or of a whole world, does not in itself have anything creative about it. Nobody can extort a new creation through the destruction of the present world. This is the fatal error of terrorists.

The true end of this world is only the side we see when God's new world begins. Just as we understand the resurrection of the dead Christ as a divine process of transformation from mortality to immortality and from shame to glory, so we can also imagine the passing away of the old and the coming of the new world as a divine transformation process. Nothing of what is will be annihilated, but everything will be transformed. "*Vita mutatur, non tollitur*," as the preface to the Roman Catholic requiem Mass says. The children in the concentration camp of Theresienstadt, in the face of their death, painted butterflies: When the poor caterpillar dies, the beautiful butterfly is born and will fly into freedom.

Christian theology answers apocalyptic questions about the end with the recollecting making-present of the crucified and risen Christ. That is the only answer we can give with the assurance of faith and without uncertain speculations. It does not answer all the apocalyptic *why*-questions about God's justice and the *when*-questions about the coming of the end. After all, Christ himself died not with an answer but with a question: "My God, why have you forsaken me?" But in the fellowship with the crucified Christ and in the real presence of the risen one, we can live with unanswered "final questions," without proffering hasty and premature answers, and without sinking answerless into brooding despondency.

Ideas about the end of history can be distinguished according to whether they deal with the goal of history (*telos*) or history's end (*finis*). If world history has a predetermined goal that then is its completion, and history moves in progress forward stage by stage—or dispensation by dispensation—in the direction of this goal. According to the biblical traditions, a goal of world history is the reign of the Son of Man (Daniel 7), or the thousand-year kingdom, where Christ, with those who are his, will rule in peace over the nations (Rev. 20). According to the notion held in the ancient world, the goal of world history is the Golden Age, which was to follow the Iron Age in history (Virgil). According to the hope of modernity, it is the realm of freedom or of eternal peace (Kant). For Francis Fukuyama (at that time an official in the U.S. State Department), after socialism collapsed in 1989, capitalism and liberal democracy—that is, the modern Western world—became this "end of history." We call ideas of this kind about the end as the goal of history *chiliastic* or *millenarian*, and if they influence the present, *messianic*. If, on the other hand, world history reaches its end in the end of the world, then it will be broken off through catastrophes. According to biblical traditions, this is "the downfall of the world" (German: *Weltuntergang*); according to the notion held in antiquity, it is "the universal conflagration" (German: *Weltenbrand*); according to modern fears, it is nuclear annihilation, or a worldwide ecological catastrophe, or destruction by terrorists. In modern parlance we call ideas of this kind *apocalyptic*. The end of the world they envisage does not structure the course of world history; in fact, it withdraws meaning from every epoch in history. World history is a meaningless history of suffering; its end is the best thing about it.

Modern faith in progress and globalization is a secularized form of the religious salvation-history millenarianism,

while modern fears about the end of the world and about
its annihilation are secularizations of the apocalyptic of
old. And in every secularization of the religious, something gets lost, and the result is also a deformation.

As we know, history is always a struggle for power. People who have power have an interest in the progress of
history and the globalization of their power. They understand the future as continuation of their own present.
People who are oppressed and powerless, set back and
insulted, have no interest in the progress and continuation
of their history of suffering. They are only interested in a
speedy end for this world and in an alternative future. So
we must also confront the different ideas about a goal or
end of history with the critical question: *Cui bono?* Whom
does it serve?

The Goal of History: Globalization

No hope has fascinated people as much as the image of a
thousand-year reign of peace, and none has caused so
much havoc. Christians expect Christ's kingdom of peace,
Romans awaited the Golden Age, modern men and
women look for "the ends of history" in a world condition
without history and without conflicts.

The first Christian fulfillment of this hope presented
itself in the astonishing turn of events under the Roman
emperor Constantine, when persecuted Christianity
became first a legal religion in the Roman Empire and
then, under the emperors Theodosius and Justinian,
Rome's all-dominating imperial religion. "Those who
have suffered with Christ will reign with him," was the
promise of the apostle Paul (2 Tim. 2:12) and "the saints
will judge the world" (1 Cor. 6:2). With this in mind, the
political turn of events was interpreted millennially as the

turn from martyrdom to millennium. The Holy Roman Empire was praised as Christ's millennium of peace. The Christian emperors saw their religious mandate in the conversion of the nations through their subjugation to Christ's end-time kingdom of peace. There is one *Pantocrator* in heaven, and his image on earth is the one Christian Caesar and his undivided, universal world monarchy.

The political theology of this universal Christian world monarchy springs from the application of the so-called image of monarchies in the seventh chapter of Daniel: Four bestial and violent empires rise up out of the sea of chaos. But at the end the humane kingdom of the divine Son of Man descends from heaven to bring everlasting peace, righteousness, and justice on earth. The fourth bestial empire was the empire of Rome, which followed the Babylonian, Persian, and Greek empires. With the Christianization of the Roman Empire, the end-time kingdom of Christ begins. This will reach to the ends of the earth and to the end of time. This formed the messianism of the Christian empire, the Christian world, and the Christian age of humankind.

The fulfillment of the same messianic hope assumed another form in the epochal consciousness of what we call "modern times" (German: *Neuzeit*). "Modern times" are the "Third Age" of humanity, as the philosophers of the Enlightenment called their present, applying the prophecy of the twelfth-century Italian visionary Joachim of Fiore of a coming "third age of the Spirit" to their own epoch. "New time" is always the end-time too, for after the new time nothing can come but the end of time. This modern epochal self-consciousness led to the idea that the European domination of the world is indeed the messianic fulfillment of world history.

A present-day form of this fulfillment is "America." The United States is a product of the Enlightenment and the firstfruits of the modern world. "America" was and is for the millions of immigrants "the New World," where freedom reigns for everyone. There are messianic elements built into the "American Dream" and consequently in American politics. The seal of the United States bears the promise "the New World Order" (*novus ordo seclorum*). What it says is not only a new world order but *the* New World Order. Just as the European ideas of modern times as the "New Time," the American "New World Order" is universal in its intention; it is a new age for humanity and a new order for the whole world.

What is the role of America in the world today? Henry Luce called the twentieth century "the American century," and he was right. The United States decided by intervention the two World Wars, and after the downfall of the Soviet empire in 1989 is the only remaining superpower. But there is more in it: While the communist experiment—forming out of many nations the new "Sovietman"—has failed, the American experiment is still going on and is going well. America is a country of immigrants from all the nations of the world: *e pluribus unum*. Regardless how well this is working inside, America is by immigration the central land of humankind and continues to be so. This means that the American experiment is an experiment of humankind and not only of Americans. The peoples of the world are waiting for the fulfillment of the original promise of America for the world: *novus ordo seclorum*. This New World Order cannot be an American world empire, but only the universal realization of the declaration that "all human beings," and not only American human beings, "are created equal." This is the vision of a world order based on human rights and the rights of nature, as the declarations of the United Nations proclaim.

The last prophet of the Western "end of history" for a time had been Francis Fukuyama. As a supporter of the undoubtedly strange interpretation of Hegel put forward by the Russian philosopher Alexandre Kojeve in Paris, he saw the "end of history" dawning with the collapse of socialism in the Soviet empire. It is the triumph of the West, he maintained, that since 1989 there has no longer been any real alternative to Western capitalism and liberal democracy. In pluralistic capitalist democracy, humanity has finally found what it was seeking for in all its social experiments. We now live for the first time in "a world without alternative." What was once living history, full of destructive but also creative conflicts, can now only be visited in history museums.

Fukuyama's "end of history" was an illusion. The protest of people ground down and humiliated, and the protest of a violated earth, will not leave the world in the condition in which it is now. According to Hegel, the sign of the "end of history" is not the lack of an alternative but freedom from contradiction. September 11, 2001, brought a terrible "end of the end of History" to all of us. The year 1989 was indeed the end of the East-West conflict and the Cold War, and the illusion of a world without alternative brought many to the idea that now globalization of what we want and what we are is at stake. Many spoke of "one world," the global village, the world community, the civilized world, and so forth. The globalization of production and markets, finance and big business, communication systems and modern culture, however, did not bring peace to the world, but produced more and more conflicts. Neoliberal, aggressive capitalism is producing inequality, while democracy is based on equality. The universal task is "to save the world for democracy." If we want peace we need a globalization of justice and respect. Otherwise we will never reach "the new world order," but only a world of chaos and terror. Only a just order can be an order for a humanity united in peace.

The End of the World: Terrorism

The fear of a catastrophic end of the world is very often merely the reverse side of the hope for the glorious fulfillment of its history. When that hope collapses, generally all that is left is this fear.

In the biblical traditions, there were not only prophetic hopes; there were always apocalyptic prophecies too. We talk about apocalypses when prophetic prophecies reach out beyond Israel's future and take on a worldwide political scope, or even cosmic dimensions. Then a "new age" of humankind or a new creation of the cosmos is promised. According to Daniel 7, a worldwide humane kingdom of the Son of Man is promised. According to the book of *1 Enoch*, "this earth will be smashed to pieces and everything upon it will be destroyed, and a judgment will come upon all." Afterwards, "the throne of God will be visible," "the Son of Man will come," and heaven and earth "will be created anew" (54:4).

The biblical apocalypses about a threatened doomsday of the world (German: *Weltuntergang*) go back to the story about Noah's flood (Gen. 6–9), according to which God decided to destroy human beings together with the earth, because of the wickedness of the powerful and the evil in human hearts, in order then with the one just man Noah, who is saved from the downfall, to make his new covenant, in which no new end of the world is envisaged (Gen. 9:11). But behind this remembered fear of the end of the world is the still more profound fear about God, the fear that

God could "repent," be sorry and regret having created human beings at all, and that God could withdraw his creative resolve altogether. A God who turns away completely leaves the world to sink into chaos and nothingness.

In distinction from the Bible's apocalyptic traditions, the phrase "apocalypse now" is used today to describe man-made catastrophes: a nuclear catastrophe, an ecological catastrophe, or a terrorist catastrophe. Apocalyptic interpretations of human crimes are, however, completely wrong, because they push off onto God that for which human beings are responsible. Human beings have to take responsibility for crimes against humanity and crimes against nature. The biblical apocalyptic traditions are full of hope, while the self-annihilation of the human race and the annihilation of the living space of this earth are pure exterminism without any hope.

It is not surprising that today the apocalyptic interpretation of crimes against humanity that threaten us all are producing a new apocalyptic terrorism. It is only a short step from passive expectation of the world's end to an active ending of it. This is the anarchism of old of which we know. In the nineteenth century, Michael Bakunin, the father of Russian anarchism, proclaimed the slogan: "The pleasure in destroying is also a creative pleasure," and with this motto justified the murder of czars and the suicide of terrorists. "Without destruction there can be no construction" was Mao Tse-tung's command to the cultural revolutionaries in China. The Cultural Revolution cost millions of people their lives and reduced China's finest cultural monuments to rubble. In Cambodia, the mass murderer Pol Pot took Mao's motto seriously. His Khmer Rouge murdered the older generations so as to build a "new world" with the young. They left behind two million dead in the killing fields, and a devastated country.

Apocalyptic terrorism can lead to the mass suicide of sect adherents: In 1978 in Jonestown, Guayana, it was 912 people belonging to a People's Temple sect; in 1993 in Waco, Texas, 78 adherents of a Branch Davidian sect, and 52 members of an end-of-the-world sect in Vietnam; in 1995, 53 members of a Sun Temple sect in Canada and Switzerland; in 1997, 39 adherents of a UFO death cult in San Diego; more recently in Uganda, hundreds killed themselves or were killed in a Catholic apocalyptic Holy Mary cult.

Apocalyptic terrorism can also lead to mass murder of other people for the sake of a better future. Genghis Khan felt called to mass murder as "the retribution of God": "I am the revenger of God" he told the people of Sarmarkand before the massacres began. The poison gas sect of Shoko Asahara in Japan 1998 apparently believed itself to be called to the final apocalyptic battle.

Since September 11, 2001, we are confronted with a new type of apocalyptic terrorism. The suicide–mass murder at the World Trade Center in New York and the Pentagon in Washington was a shock to many. These acts have led me to the following observations:

1. One may become a murderer for money or out of conviction, but a suicide-murderer only out of conviction. The new terrorists are neither sick nor desperados, but radical Islamists in a demonic way. They act believing they are martyrs of their faith, and are revered by their families and peer groups.

2. What kind of conviction motivates them? For decades the United States has been accused by fanatic masses in some Islamic cities as "the great Satan," and the Western world as the wicked home of the infidels for its secularism, materialism, pornography, family breakdowns, drug dependency, women's liberation, and so forth. "The

great Satan" is nothing else than the apocalyptic enemy of God. Whoever weakens and humiliates him is on God's side and earns paradise.

3. The idea to fight with God in the final battle against God's enemies takes away any inhibition on killing people, elevates the ecstasy of power, and turns suicide into a divine service. These Islamist suicide-terrorists must feel like God destroying the godless. Because they feel like divine executioners, they need no justification for their mass murder. The meaning of their terrorism is terror, nothing else.

4. Islamist terrorism is not terrorism out of oppression and starvation. These terrorists come from good families in rich countries in the Near East, not out of the slums of Africa or Asia. The motivation must lie in a special kind of hitherto unknown Islamist apocalypticism and in the old Islamic assassin tradition from the tenth century.

No God and no religion can justify this new suicide–mass murder. Can it be a sign of strong faith to become a mass murderer? No. Is this apocalyptic in the biblical sense? No. The biblical apocalypses have nothing to do with these kinds of apocalyptic terrorism. On the contrary, they keep hope alive for God's faithfulness to his creatures in the terrors of the end-time: "Who endures until the end, will be saved." "When these things begin to take place, stand up and raise your heads, because your redemption is drawing near" (Luke 21:28). Prophetic hope is *hope in action*. Apocalyptic hope is *hope in danger*, a hope that is capable of suffering—a patient, enduring, and resistant hope.

Hope Is the Last to Die

Looking now to the future, I am led to make the following observations:

1. Christian hope is the power to begin a new life. "In my end is my beginning." We understand standing up after failure and starting anew. What is more difficult is to stand up and start anew after success. The development of the modern Western world is a success story of the scientific-technological mind. Its globalization after 1989 into "one world" was very successful—for us, but unfortunately not for everybody. The ghastly ditch between the First World and the Third World was deepened, and millions of home-less migrants are wandering around, knocking at the doors of rich countries. The mortality rates for children in Africa are growing. The losers of globalization are crying out for their right to life and to freedom. We must, I believe, start a new globalization: a global action against poverty and hunger, a global liberation from oppression, and a global respect for cultural identity. Globalization for tomorrow means the renunciation of the arrogance of power in the Western world and a solidarity in compassion with the wounded and suffering people on earth.

2. Dialogue between the world's religions is necessary, but not the problem of the day. A "clash between civiliza-tions" is not the challenge we are facing. The "war" that has come over us since September 11, 2001, is the terror-istic reaction of a radical wing of Islamic fundamentalism against the desires of the modern world for a peaceful life among different religious communities in a common civil society. Religious communities can live in the modern world under three conditions:

1. the separation of church and state, or religious and civil community;
2. individual religious freedom;
3. dignity and human rights for women.

Modern Islam, or the Islam in modern societies, has agreed to these conditions and has given up the *sharia* (the Islamic legal system) and *jihad* (in the sense of "holy war"). Fundamentalist Islam, on the contrary, is a reaction against these three conditions of the modern world. They want a Muslim state with the exclusion of non-Muslims and the subjection of women. They want to revitalize for this goal the *sharia* and call for a *jihad* against the modern states in the Western and also in the Arab world.

There are only a few countries in the world where those three conditions of the modern world are not accepted. Members of the United Nations have to live up to them.

The modern world is an open world, as discussions about postmodernism or the ecological revolution show. But it can offer peace between religious communities only under the three conditions mentioned, because these three were the conditions for overcoming the religious wars in Europe in the seventeenth century. They gave birth to the modern world. They are essential for the modernization of the world today.

3. "The hope of the people dies last." I first heard this utterance many years ago in Brazil, and then it resurfaced in August 2002 as people on the Elbe and Mulde Rivers struggled to protect their homes against Germany's biggest flood in living memory, sometimes successfully, sometimes in vain.

If we take this bold saying in a positive sense, then it must mean that hope survives everything—the floods and the dikes, the successes and the failures, the presumption and the despair—for everything that is alive lives from hope. Hope keeps us alive because it is itself a power of life. It helps us to survive the defeats and disruptions of our lives. *Dum spiro spero*, goes a Latin proverb: As long as

I have breath, I hope. The reverse is also true: As long as I hope, I have breath.

Will this hope of our lives really die last, or will we not rather in this hope itself become immortal because hope and what we hope for also survive our death?

If life ends in nothing more than dying and death, then the good-byes we experience in life will have the upper hand, for in that case everything we experience is transitory and passes away. But if the leave-taking of Jesus in his death led to the new beginning of his resurrection, then we also will find in our end the new beginning, the beginning of eternal life. Thus, the new beginnings in this life are already more important for us than the leave-takings. In the rebirth of a living hope, already here and now, we come near to the primal power of life that encounters us in death as the power of resurrection. Death is the end but not the last. The last is eternal life in the glory of God.

Selected Bibliography

Jürgen Moltmann and Elisabeth Moltmann-Wendel

God—His and Hers. Trans. John Bowden. New York: Crossroad, 1991.
Humanity in God. New York: Pilgrim Press, 1983.

Elisabeth Moltmann-Wendel

Autobiography. Trans. John Bowden. London: SCM Press, 1997.
I Am My Body: A Theology of Embodiment. Trans. John Bowden. New York: Continuum, 1995.
A Land Flowing with Milk and Honey: Perspectives on Feminist Theology. Trans. John Bowden. New York: Crossroad, 1986.
Liberty, Equality, Sisterhood: On the Emancipation of Women in Church and Society. Trans. Ruth Gritsch. Philadelphia: Fortress Press, 1978.
Rediscovering Friendship: Awakening to the Power and Promise of Women's Friendships. Trans. John Bowden. Minneapolis: Fortress Press, 2001.

Jürgen Moltmann

The Church in the Power of the Spirit. Trans. Margaret Kohl. New York: Harper & Row, 1967.
The Coming of God: Christian Eschatology. Trans. Margaret Kohl. Minneapolis: Fortress Press, 1996.
The Crucified God: The Cross of Christ as the Foundation and Criticism of Christian Theology. Trans. R. A. Wilson and John Bowden. New York: Harper & Row, 1974.
Experiences in Theology: Ways and Forms of Christian Theology. Trans. Margaret Kohl. Minneapolis: Fortress Press, 2000.
The Future of Creation. Trans. Margaret Kohl. Philadelphia: Fortress Press, 1979.

God in Creation: An Ecological Doctrine of Creation. Trans. Margaret Kohl. San Francisco: Harper & Row, 1985.

History and the Triune God: Contributions to Trinitarian Theology. New York: Crossroad, 1982.

On Human Dignity: Political Theology and Ethics. Trans. and with an introduction by M. Douglas Meeks. Philadelphia: Fortress Press, 1984.

The Passion for Life: A Messianic Lifestyle. Trans. and with an introduction by M. Douglas Meeks. Philadelphia: Fortress Press, 1978.

The Spirit of Life: A Universal Affirmation. Trans. Margaret Kohl. Minneapolis: Fortress Press, 1992.

The Trinity and the Kingdom: The Doctrine of God. Trans. Margaret Kohl. San Francisco: Harper & Row, 1981.

The Way of Jesus Christ: Christology in Messianic Dimensions. Trans. Margaret Kohl. San Francisco: HarperSanFrancisco, 1990.

Theology of Hope: On the Ground and the Implications of a Christian Eschatology. Trans. James W. Leitch. New York: Harper & Row, 1967.

DATE DUE

The Library Store   #47-0103